GARDENS *for* PLEASURE

Dedication

For Jon, Kelsey and Arquie

GARDENS *for* PLEASURE

Brodee Myers-Cooke

Angus&Robertson
An imprint of HarperCollins*Publishers*

Acknowledgments

··

I would sincerely like to thank the following people who generously gave their help and support during the writing of this book: Jon Cooke, Trevor and Shen Myers, Dallas and Kevin Fell, Bronte and Kendall Waller, Ron and Norma Cooke, Tony Shannon, Philippa Scarf, Margaret Whiskin, Lucy Tumanow-West, Kerry Klinner, Sue Grose-Hodge, Ngaire Wills, Leslye Cole, Angus Stewart, Rodger Elliot, Louise Johnston; and Chris Samarajiwa, Knowhow Solutions, Rose Bay, NSW; Philip Moore, Renaissance Herbs, Warnervale, NSW; Tim North, Australian Garden Journal, Manuka, ACT; Nik Romanowski, Dragonfly Aquatics, Colac, Victoria; and David Glenn, Lambley Nursery, Ascot, Victoria. Outside Australia, the following people kindly assisted in providing information: David Barker, The Hardy Plant Society, UK; Craig Tufts, National Wildlife Federation, Washington, D.C., USA; Paul Chambers, Australian Native Landscapes Co., Phoenix, Arizona, USA; Ron Gass, Mountain States Wholesale Nursery, Glendale, Arizona, USA; Jeff Rosendale, Rosendale Nursery, Watsonville, California, USA; Victor C. Yool, Berkeley Horticultural Nursery, Berkeley, California, USA; Danny Takao, Takao Nursery, Fresno, California, USA.

Angus&Robertson
An imprint of HarperCollins*Publishers* , Australia

First published in Australia in 1996
by HarperCollins*Publishers* Pty Limited
ACN 009 913 517
A member of the HarperCollins*Publishers* (Australia) Pty Limited Group

7/98 Gen fund 20⁰⁰

Copyright © Brodee Myers-Cooke 1996

HarperCollins*Publishers*
25 Ryde Road, Pymble, Sydney, NSW 2073, Australia
31 View Road, Glenfield, Auckland 10, New Zealand
77–85 Fulham Palace Road, London W6 8JB, United Kingdom
Hazelton Lanes, 55 Avenue Road, Suite 2900, Toronto, Ontario M5R 3L2
and 1995 Markham Road, Scarborough, Ontario M1B 5M8 Canada
10 East 53rd Street, New York NY 10032, USA

National Library of Australia Cataloguing-in-Publication data:

Myers-Cooke, Brodee, 1961 — .
Gardens for pleasure: designs, ideas and inspiration.
Bibliography.
Includes index.

ISBN 0 207 18901 3.
1. Gardens — Design. 2. Gardening. 3. Landscape gardening. I. Title.
712.6

Cover and internal illustrations by Brodee Myers-Cooke

Printed in Hong Kong

9 8 7 6 5 4 3 2 1
00 99 98 97 96

Contents

Introduction

When I close my eyes, I can return to a favourite garden from my childhood. I am sitting on a 'swing' of wisteria vine which swoops almost to the ground, crushing fragrant flowers between my fingers, beneath the spreading arms of an old man banksia tree. I remember every scent and sound, every shaft of sunlight of this gentle experience. I don't know why my memory chose to capture this moment in its cupped hands, but I'm glad it did, because it constantly reminds me what gardens are all about — they are about *experiences*.

Too often we are encouraged to think of the garden as little more than a pretty picture. But the best gardens have much more: they stir something deeper than visual pleasure. They beckon us to touch and sing songs to us. They are alive — with other living things ... and with possibilities as well. They calm and delight, and entice us with secrets we need to unravel.

The options for an outdoor space, no matter how small, are vast and exciting, yet many of the most luxurious and enticing possibilities are rarely considered. This book offers ideas, inspiration and information which, I hope, will set you on the path to your own dream garden. At the very least I hope it will make you throw your door open and take a fresh look around — to see your garden's potential to thrill, amuse, excite, treat, titillate, gratify, luxuriate and refresh, its potential for idyllic bliss, and for adventures, bold and simple.

The first section of this book, 'Sensory Pleasure Gardens', is an armchair guide to just some of the pleasurable themes which are possible in our gardens. Each of the senses, apart from sight, are considered in turn, then the Night Garden shows one way to bring them together for sensuous rhapsody. The second section, 'Living Pleasure Gardens', shows how to lure butterflies, birds and other animals to your garden for a spontaneous theatre of living things, 'Passive Pleasure Gardens' considers restorative open-air spaces for the body and soul and 'Interactive Pleasure Gardens' takes you on a wander through gardens that are functional, or just plain fun.

Each chapter includes a detailed garden plan and 'guided tour' of a large garden where a specific pleasure can be enjoyed. It is my hope that you may enter these imaginary worlds and live each one for awhile — to swing in the hammock beneath the stars, and hop from stepping stone to stepping stone to your own deserted island. Imagining you are there should help you to decide whether to include such a plan, or at least certain elements of it, in your own garden.

This large plan is followed by a plan, notes and ideas for small and tiny garden spaces. These contain plenty of fresh design solutions for tight spaces in larger gardens, too — such as neglected corners, balconies, verandahs and window boxes.

'Landscaping Your Garden' looks at how landscape elements such as paths, lawns, walls and fences can add further relish to the garden. The premise here is: never sacrifice function for beauty, but by all means make it pleasurable. The last section of the book, 'The Pleasure Plant Index' is a guide to some of the world's most bewitching species. It begins with the 'Key Guide', a design tool to help you weave many themes into a single outdoor space. This is followed by 'Descriptions', which includes all you need to know about flowering season, colour, height and growing conditions.

In both the 'Pleasure Plant Index' and the garden plans, preference has been given to plants which are beautiful, adaptable and easily grown in a vast range of conditions.

How to Use this Book

All the plans are designed to get you started on your own ideas; they are not intended to be copied slavishly. Besides, each is for a hypothetical area of large, open, sunny space, and you may not have

such an area waiting to be filled in your garden. But, whatever your patch of outdoor space is like, you may be surprised by what is possible.

The art of gardening is about adaptation — of taking ideas and twisting them to suit your tastes, conditions and existing features. The best approach is to couple your own brainstorming with expert advice. A local nursery person, qualified horticulturist or landscape contractor should be able to tell you which plants are suitable for both your climate and your chosen location, and they may be able to suggest alternatives for those which are not. A landscape contractor can also provide design solutions for difficult areas and sloping sites.

If you use the large colour plans as a guide for your own designs, it is important to note the position of the sun on the plan. This indicates north in the Southern Hemisphere and south in the Northern Hemisphere. As you are probably aware, this affects the sun and shadow patterns throughout the garden, especially when siting large shrubs and trees.

A Note About Gardening

Healthy, thriving plants will undoubtedly increase the pleasure your garden brings, so I would like to pass on the two most important lessons I have learned about gardening. The first is: never stop improving your soil with compost, mulch and organic fertilizers. Every effort you lavish on your soil is an investment in the health of your garden, and the enjoyment it brings. The second lesson is: know your garden's climate and conditions — especially its limitations — and work with them rather than against them. You may lack sun, or suffer from drought or heavy frosts, but, whatever the conditions, there are beautiful pleasure plants tailor-made for your garden.

Sensory Pleasure Gardens

WEEPING
MULBERRY

GRAPE
TUNNEL

STRAWBERRY
PATCH

BLUEBERRY

NASTURTIUM

BORAGE

SUNFLOWERS

FENNEL

PASSIONFRUIT

THYME

BANANAS

MANDARIN

HERBS

TOMATO

ORANGE

LEMON

LIME

CARROTS

GALANGAL

ESPALIERED
FRUIT
TREES

MACADAMIA

PEACH

KIWIFRUIT

Chapter 1

The Listening Garden

Here will we sit, and let the sounds of music
Creep in our ears.

William Shakespeare (1564–1616), *The Merchant of Venice*

When the eyesight of renowned garden designer and writer Gertrude Jekyll began to fail, her ears, at times, became her eyes. Sitting in her garden she was able to distinguish one bird from another from the sound of wings overhead, and she delighted in the sound of leaves — how the voice of each tree changed with the winds and seasons.

Could it be that those of us lucky enough to have full sight would get more from our gardens if we used our eyes less? Why not wander the garden with your ears, and let the gate to a secret garden creak open: using your ears for flight, look into the crevices where skinks scuffle, climb into thickets where birds ruffle their young, soar to the top of a tree, then dip your toe in a tinkling fountain nearby.

Whether we are lying on our backs letting sounds wash over us like waves, or sitting with our eyes fixed on the pages of a book, our ears are gloriously free to roam. A garden of sounds can sail through the window to join us for breakfast and newspapers in bed. Even when we are barely aware of the existence of sound, and only our subconscious has one ear pricked, sound affects our state of mind.

The dimension of sound deserves consideration in every garden — even if it is an interesting side dish to the main course, or a little seasoning and spice sprinkled on the top. The creative possibilities are endless, and the territory largely unexplored.

Start by sharpening your awareness. Search out as many sounds as you can, and take note of how they make you feel. Sound, like taste, is a matter of preference, so sampling is a springboard to the best ideas. Go forth like a pioneer, with the following map of what we know so far.

First, there are birds — without a doubt the star performers of the Listening Garden. Think about the wealth of possibilities in birdsong: coos, trills, warbles, chirps, tweets, twitters, clucks, squawks, crows, gobbles, quacks and honks, night calls and daytime songs. The right garden ingredients will entice these songsters to your door.

But it's not all song — there's dance too, like the beat of wings in flight, and chickens scratching. Add the jazzy undertones of bees and buzzing insects, and husky solos by frogs, crickets and cicadas, and you have a unique jam session.

Apart from luring all the songsters, plants play their own part in the ensemble as the percussion section that beats out the rhythm of the wind and rain. Each sings, murmurs, rattles and rustles, as Gertrude Jekyll noted, with a voice of its own, pianissimo or fortissimo depending on the weather. It has been said that the giant reed (*Arundo donax*) 'whispers in the breeze and is silent in the storm'.

Trees provide a background accompaniment to the symphony, and a fragrant tree that is admired for its beauty and which also pleases the ear will be doubly treasured. Include at least one deciduous tree for the joy of crushing leaves beneath your feet.

Large-leafed plants, such as bananas, cannas and *Alocasia* have double value: in a breeze their leaves clap together, and in rain their leaf surfaces become the skin of a drum. In cooler zones try hostas, *Gunnera manicata*, *Ligularia dentata*, and the hardy palm *Trachycarpus fortunei*. If kept in pots, the Abyssinian banana plant (*Ensete ventricosum*) and cannas can be brought indoors for winter.

Of the smaller plants, grasses and bamboo are the most lyrical. In fact, the melodious qualities of bamboo have captivated poets and writers for centuries. In his book *Gardens and People*, American landscape architect Fletcher Steele says bamboo transports the ear 'to Fairyland with the sweetest, strangest music in Titania's repertoire'.

But not all grasses are effective sound-makers; species with dry, strap-like leaves are often the best. When shopping around, give the plants a gentle shake to choose a grass that's as songful as it is beautiful, and search out plants with seeds that rattle and shake. Many varieties of poppy, including the opium poppy (*Papaver somniferum*), have seed heads that shake like maracas. Those of honesty (*Lunaria annua*) clap together like tiny castanets.

Of all the elements in the Listening Garden, moving water is the most potent and bewitching. It generates so many moods, and comes in so many forms. Draw your inspiration from the mood and terrain of the garden — a waterfall is ideal for a sloping site in a natural setting, whereas fountains are suited to formal gardens. Grand settings deserve an equally grand water feature, while intimate spots need a subtle approach.

Next we come to accessories such as wind chimes, which range from tinkling bells to the dulcet, almost bluesy, tones of hand-tuned pipes. The power of the sound of wind chimes as a mood-setter cannot be underestimated, so choose and position the chimes with great care.

Rain can also be harnessed for sound effects in the Listening Garden; build a place to go during rainstorms and downpours — somewhere with a metal roof and a pond in front for added acoustics.

Here we reach the end of the map, but the best route to a Listening Garden is to become a connoisseur of sound. All you need do is tune in.

Plan for a Listening Garden

The entrance to the Listening Garden is between two bold clumps of shoulder-high zebra grass (*Miscanthus sinensis* 'Zebrinus'). With its graceful upright foliage, this grass shivers and shakes and waves its gold-patterned leaves like festive streamers.

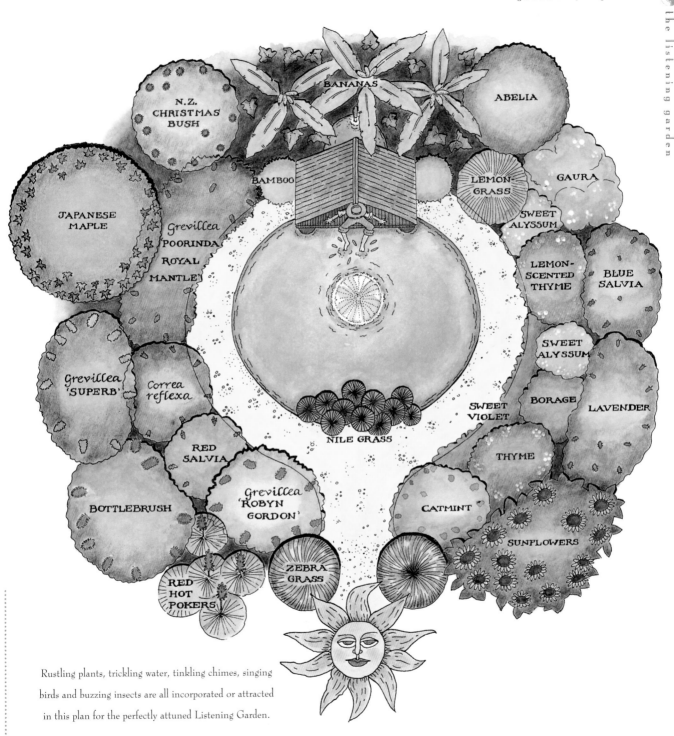

BANANAS

N.Z. CHRISTMAS BUSH

ABELIA

BAMBOO

LEMON-GRASS

GAURA

JAPANESE MAPLE

Grevillea POORINDA ROYAL MANTLE'

SWEET ALYSSUM

LEMON-SCENTED THYME

BLUE SALVIA

Grevillea 'SUPERB'

Correa reflexa

SWEET ALYSSUM

BORAGE

LAVENDER

RED SALVIA

SWEET VIOLET

NILE GRASS

THYME

BOTTLEBRUSH

Grevillea 'ROBYN GORDON'

CATMINT

SUNFLOWERS

RED HOT POKERS

ZEBRA GRASS

Rustling plants, trickling water, tinkling chimes, singing birds and buzzing insects are all incorporated or attracted in this plan for the perfectly attuned Listening Garden.

11

Once inside, a pebble path leads right and left skirting a circular pond and leading to a small open-sided pavilion. Ahead, the upturned broom-heads of Nile grass (*Cyperus papyrus*) gently swish the air. To the left are nectar-rich, red-flowering plants such as salvia, red hot poker (*Kniphofia*), New Zealand Christmas bush (*Metrosideros excelsa*) and Australian natives such as grevillea, bottlebrush (*Callistemon*) and *Correa reflexa*. Birds find these irresistible and fly down from the Japanese maple (*Acer palmatum*) nearby. *Grevillea* 'Robyn Gordon' in particular is a bird magnet. Its flower, which looks like an exploding firecracker, literally drips with honey.

Japanese maple fits perfectly into this setting. A deciduous tree, it provides delicate crunching leaves in autumn, yet is compact enough for most gardens. And the leaves pitter-patter in the breeze like fairy footsteps. In his book *The 500 Best Garden Plants*, British writer Patrick Taylor describes the Japanese maple as 'irresistibly glamorous'. It prefers a climate with warm clear days and cool crisp nights, in a place protected from harsh winds.

If the local conditions are less than ideal, search out another suitable tree for your Listening Garden because, for precious birdsong, a tree's presence is the thing. While smaller food plants ensure bird visits, a tree encourages them to linger and sing their songs.

The garden to the right of the pond is a-buzz with bee plants. Whereas birds are attracted to the red spectrum, blues bring bees and other insects, so on the right side of the pond a blue and white theme dominates, with a splash of gold here and there. Plants such as sweet violet, thyme, sweet alyssum, borage and catmint (*Nepeta* x *faassenii*), topple over the path, with lavender, gaura, blue salvia and sunflowers behind. Tuneful strap-leafed plants such as lemon grass and ribbon grass (*Phalaris arundinacea* var. *picta*) are in good company here. Nearby, abelia provides a thicket for birds.

Bamboo in large pots rustles and creaks either side of the pavilion. Behind, a trickle of water from a bamboo fluke dances into a semicircular basin before running under the pavilion via a cobbled stream. The basin is surrounded by large-leafed plants, such as palms and bananas or, in cool climates, *Ligularia dentata*.

Restful-toned wind chimes hang from the pavilion which rests its front piers in the pond. With a bench-seat or hammock it is a sanctuary in a storm, when rain plays its xylophone on the roof and pond, and the large leaves behind become a timpani. On clear days it is a sun-drenched pier on which to sit and splash the water with your feet and listen to the tune of the central fountain.

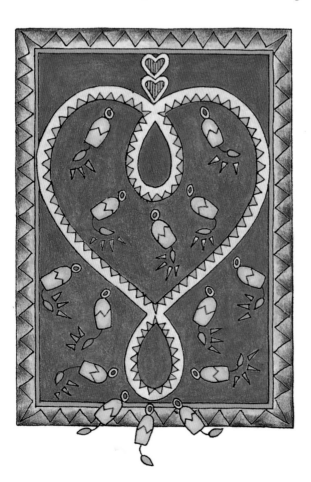

A Smaller Listening Garden

For a smaller, but no less sound-filled version of the Listening Garden, create a clearing where waving grasses wrap around a bench-seat with bee and bird plants either side. If space allows, the trickling water feature with bamboo fluke doubles as a shallow basin where birds can come to splash.

Make full use of vertical space. Look around for places which reach high for available breezes, and be aware of wind patterns around your garden. Use brackets, pegs and hooks to attach sound-makers to fences, walls and archways. Make a totem pole where harmonising wind chimes sing a constant roundelay. For added sound effects, floor the area with pea gravel.

As with all Listening Gardens, there are three particularly good locations: a wind-exposed area; near the house, so that it can be enjoyed from inside as well as out; or in a far-away corner where the sounds will beckon you to wander.

A Tiny Listening Garden

It is possible to create a Listening Garden on a balcony or terrace: any of the smaller bee plants suggested in the large plan will grow well in pots and generate a happy drone; a few of the red-flowering bird plants shown in the large plan are also suitable for pots, particularly salvia and well-clipped *Grevillea* 'Robyn Gordon'.

For a Listening Garden outside a window, cram a window box with bee plants, such as thyme, borage, sweet alyssum and lavender, to cause a constant buzz.

Rather than stringing up the standard single wind chime, consider more creative approaches. Make use of the eaves for hanging chimes and bells. A length of wooden dowel attached by brackets to

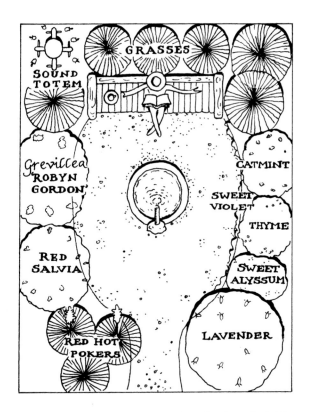

In this plan for a smaller Listening Garden, a bench-seat backed by singing grasses also has bee and bird-attracting plants on either side. A totem pole of wind chimes and a basin where water trickles from a bamboo pipe add to the music of the fauna and flora.

the outside of the window can be strung with chimes or coloured glass pieces on fine lines; the latter will tinkle and, at a sunny window, also project a kaleidoscope of colour on the floors and walls within.

Or fill a nearby tree with tiny bells. In a deciduous tree, especially, bells add interest and beauty, and they ring loudest when the tree loses its cloak of leaves. The washing line, too, gains a touch of whimsy with sound-makers strung along its length, as does a balcony railing or awning.

Chapter 2

The Fragrant Garden

Oh! bring thy couch where countless roses
The garden's gay retreat discloses,
There in the shade of waving boughs recline
Breathing rich odours, quaffing ruby wine!

Mohammed Od-din Hafez (1325–1390), a Persian poet

*I*f sound is a password to the secret world of here and now, then scent is a magic carpet. Without warning, on a waft, we're away. It may be to a place half-forgotten — an overgrown corner of a childhood garden where scent seems to hide in morning dewdrops. Or it may be to a place conjured by the imagination — where huge leaves sway overhead and fragrance swims forever on the night's balmy air.

Whether it is full-bodied and sweet, or it is luscious and fruity, fragrance is impossible to ignore. We may be too preoccupied as we go about our busy lives to notice a favourite plant's first unfurled bloom, but a scent on the breeze can make us stop in our tracks. Forgetting our appointments, we sniff the air and stomp about the garden until we find the fragrant source.

Although the range of scents is vast, our vocabulary for them is small. To compound the problem, everyone's perception is slightly different and, like taste, smell has more than one dimension. Still, grouping plants roughly according to fragrance is helpful in understanding the scent spectrum so we can use it to advantage around the garden.

So let us, just for a moment, suspend reason and imagine we could set out some of the main scents before us — pots of scent, if you like. If we popped off the lid of each in turn, peered inside and took a sniff, what would we find?

The first pot might be brimming with sweet scents: some subtle such as the rose 'Cecile Brunner', others stronger with floral notes such as sweet violet, lilac and Chinese wisteria. Rich, golden honey scents are here too, such as those of buddleia and sweet alyssum, as well as the sweet-spiced shades of jasmine, akebia, mock orange (*Philadelphus coronarius*) and winter sweet (*Chimonanthus praecox*), and pinks (*Dianthus*) and stock (*Matthiola incana*) which seem sprinkled with cloves.

Leaves fly out of the next pot — the spicy scents of basil, cardamom and curry plant (*Helichrysum angustifolium*) — conjuring images of Persia, along with the more pungent flavours of artemisia, rosemary, sage and catmint (*Nepeta* x *faassenii*).

In the next pot we find citrus and lemon-scented aromas. Some are sweet-scented flowers with a squeeze of lemon, such as magnolia, daphne, brown boronia and evening primrose (*Oenothera biennis*), but mainly we find foliage from plants in all shapes and sizes. Close to the ground are lemon-scented varieties of thyme and geranium (*Pelargonium*), in shrubs lemon-scented verbena (*Aloysia triphylla*) and lemon-scented tea tree (*Leptospermum petersonii*), and way overhead but conveniently dropping its leaves for us to crush is the lemon-scented gum (*Eucalyptus citriodora*). A final sniff reveals some sweeter citrus notes found in the leaves of orange-scented geranium.

The next pot is an olfactory fruit salad: rich and fruity freesias, *Alocasia*, *Rosa* 'Albertine', *Osmanthus fragrans*, apricot-scented gardenia and apple-scented rugosa rose 'Max Graf'. In foliage there are brown boronia and pineapple sage. There's also the delirious scent of the real thing — peaches, plums, apples, passionfruit, strawberry and blueberry.

A lolly shop leaps out of the next pot: plants such as heliotrope, *Clematis montana* and *Stanhopea* orchids with distinctive vanilla scents to be dolloped around the garden like blobs of fresh cream; aniseed-scented primroses and the Australian native aniseed tree (*Backhousia anisata*); bubble-gum flavours of Arabian and Azores jasmine (*Jasminum sambac* and *J. azoricum*, respectively); and the banana-lollipop aroma of port wine magnolia (*Michelia figo*).

'So let us, just for a moment, suspend reason and imagine we could set out some of the main scents before us — pots of scent, if you like. If we popped off the lid of each in turn, peered inside and took a sniff, what would we find?'

In the last pot on our aromatic tour we savour the delights of fresh scents: mint in all its flavours of peppermint, spearmint, applemint and eau de cologne; purple mint bush (*Prostanthera ovalifolia*), delicious peppermint-scented geranium, eucalyptus-scented geranium, many Australian eucalypts, and conifers with refreshing resinous scents. Finally, as if to clear the air, is a haunting waft-of-wilderness from camellias in flower.

This plan for a Fragrant Garden will provide a generous palette of scents and aromatic sensations all year round. Not only does it abound with fragrant flowers, but also sweet-smelling leaves, barks and resins.

Backhousia citriodora

Osmanthus fragrans

STANDARD Murraya

PINEAPPLE SAGE

THYME

POET'S JASMINE

STANDARD Gardenia

Camellia sasanqua

ORANGE

BROWN BORONIA

Jasminum polyanthum

LEMON & FRUITY SCENTS

WISTERIA

DAPHNE

AKEBIA

Rosa 'ALBERTINE'

LAVENDER

VANILLA & CLOVE SCENTS

WINTER SWEET

Rosa 'NEW DAWN'

Rosa FRU DAGMAR HASTRUP

Rosa 'MAX GRAF'

HELIOTROPE

CHINESE STAR JASMINE

PEPPER-MINT-SCENTED GERANIUM

Gardenia augusta RADICANS

PATIO ROSES

Consider this only as a starting point for the creation of your own scent palette. As you explore fragrance you will group scents in your own way, and this is half the fun. The best fragrant gardens are made by following your nose, so savour scent wherever you go and seek out fragrance in flowers, fruit, foliage, stems, bark, seeds and resins.

As you collect your favourites, remember: in the Fragrant Garden, it's not what you've got, it's the way you use it. Place subtle fragrances within easy reach of the nose — near the house, paths and other much-used places. If plants need to be crushed or brushed to bring out their scent, be sure to place them where this will happen. Sprinkle scent about every door, arch and gateway. Stronger perfumes and scents that float on air can be placed further away, but everything should be accessible. Even when the perfume is strong, you will want to sink your face into it.

Create narrow paths where thyme, scented geraniums and pennyroyal spill over the edge. Line wider paths with lavender, rosemary, pineapple sage and nutmeg bush (*Iboza riparia*). Leave gaps in the pavers where pinks and sweet alyssum can live; fill spaces in brick paving with Corsican mint; create carpets of chamomile. For special occasions, strew paths with freshly cut leaves.

Most importantly, when it comes to flowering fragrance, take your time. The most euphoric garden is planted season by season or, better still, month by month with favourite selections made on each nursery visit. Buy a little often: this is the recipe for year-round fragrance. And choose your nursery wisely; look for one that stocks old-fashioned varieties as well as the modern forms, as new-generation hybrids often lack the fragrant intensity of their parents.

Have plantings follow your seasonal movements about the garden and house. In summer, drape a gazebo with ambrosial summer-flowering

climbers — perhaps the musky-sweet rose 'Zephirine Drouhin' and Azores jasmine. In winter, choose something like daphne or winter sweet to place below the window of your favourite room.

Each season think of fragrant ways to make chores more enjoyable: have a scented autumn flowerer accompany you as you sweep leaves from the terrace; a lemon-scented gum over the lawn could make mowing a whole new experience.

Most of all, have fun with fragrance. Weave it into the garden with meaning, if you like. Stephen Lacey, in his remarkable book *The Startling Jungle*, suggests planting schemes where colour and scent conspire to create a mood. Lemon fragrance is combined with yellow tones, chocolate and peppermint with bronze and white, and sugar and spice with 'heavy velvet purples' and golds. These dynamic acts of self-expression make for an exciting garden; try some of your own and blaze a few trails.

Plan for a Fragrant Garden

The Fragrant Garden is enclosed on all sides and has a single entry through an arch. Either side of the arch is a raised brick planter where heliotrope, patio roses, prostrate *Gardenia augusta* 'Radicans' and *Rosa* 'Max Graf' spill over the edge, providing a fragrant invitation to enter.

The arch itself is smothered in Chinese star jasmine (*Trachelospermum jasminoides*) and, either side of it, two pots of peppermint-scented geranium are placed for brushing past. Inside is a large sun-drenched garden with a verdant central pergola. Heat radiates from the brick paving, activating the scent of the randomly planted mounds of thyme, golden marjoram and sweet alyssum.

To the right, past a pyramid of lavender, is a summer garden where a rose-clad arbour shades a long, wide bench. In summer, bare feet tickle a

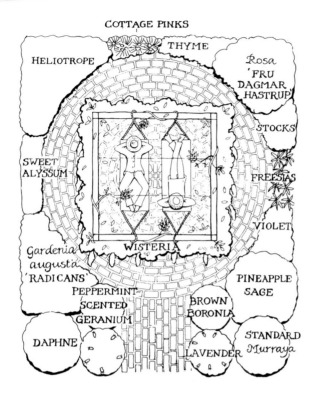

COTTAGE PINKS
THYME
HELIOTROPE
Rosa 'FRU DAGMAR HASTRUP'
STOCKS
SWEET ALYSSUM
FREESIAS
Gardenia augusta 'RADICANS'
WISTERIA
VIOLET
PEPPERMINT-SCENTED GERANIUM
PINEAPPLE SAGE
BROWN BORONIA
DAPHNE
STANDARD *Murraya*
LAVENDER

Plants for year-round fragrance surround a wisteria-clad pergola in this plan for a smaller Fragrant Garden.

rectangle of Corsican mint, spread like a rug beneath the lunch table. Fragrance fills the air with spicy-sweet *Rosa* 'Fru Dagmar Hastrup', orange-scented jessamine (*Murraya paniculata*), *Alocasia* (under the arbour's shade) and the fruity scent of *Rosa* 'Albertine' itself. Described by more than one writer as having the finest perfume of any flower, 'Albertine' floats around the entire garden. A little further on, the Australian native *Backhousia citriodora* is also in flower, but it is the foliage — an intoxicating lemon scent — we inhale as we brush past on the way to the autumn garden.

Here a trellis-backed seat clothed in poet's jasmine (*Jasminum officinale*) has Standard *Gardenia*

augusta on one side and pineapple sage within easy reach on the other. The perfume of nearby *Osmanthus fragrans* and *Camellia sasanqua* wafts about.

Moving on, past an orange tree in the corner, is a garden for winter and early spring — a sun-soaked seat with sweet-spiced daphne either side, backed by a high brick wall. The air here is infused with fragrance, and not just from sweet orange blossoms and daphne. Plants such as freesias, pinks, heliotropes and stocks fill two island beds nearby, one with lemon and fruity scents, the other with vanilla and cloves. In a pot under the orange tree, a brown boronia is both fruity and lemon at once in its foliage and flowers. The wall is a colourful mural where *Jasminum polyanthum*, akebia and *Rosa* 'New Dawn' mingle flowers, leaves and scents.

A pergola in the middle of the garden, draped in Chinese wisteria, is for year-round pleasure. Its central location means it picks up the strongest scents from all corners of the garden, including that of winter sweet. Large hanging baskets change with the seasons — during summer, pinks and lilies; in autumn, gardenia and heliotrope; in winter, daphne and freesias; and, in spring, brown boronia and bulbs such as fragrant jonquils and daffodils.

Beneath the pergola, a pair of hammocks bask in winter sun and shelter under summer's leafy cover. In spring long lavender-blue racemes tumble from the roof, as if to touch the nose.

A Smaller Fragrant Garden

Each seasonal garden within the larger Fragrant Garden plan is self-contained and, as such, can be accomplished independently by choosing areas around the garden appropriate for particular seasons. Alternatively, select a few plants from each of the plan's seasonal gardens to create a miniature year-round Fragrant Garden.

Where space is limited, beware of large plants that flower only fleetingly.

Once you have planted the scents you adore, continue planting your favourites, but try to choose smaller-growing, clippable and longer-flowering plants over others.

Many of the most popular scented plants are available in topiarised form; among these, standards are perfect for a small Fragrant Garden. Resembling living lollipops with a ball of foliage and flowers atop a long, bare stem, standard plants bring aroma to where we want it — right under our noses.

Make good use of foliage plants for year-round fragrance and place them in accessible spots. Either side of an often-used flight of steps, for instance, is an ideal place for a collection of sweet-scented geraniums, or thymes in terracotta pots.

Some of the most valuable fragrant plants for the terrace or patio are those that live happily in pots and offer a variety of fragrances within a single plant; good examples are brown boronia, purple mint bush and orange trees.

Orange trees are a particularly worthwhile plant for both terrace and balcony gardens, with sweet spring flowers and citrus-scented foliage all year round, and the juicy aroma of the oranges themselves. These ripen in winter and stay on the tree for several weeks (if you can resist eating them).

A Tiny Fragrant Garden

Outline windows and doorways with trellising or wire to support fragrant climbers if there is no room for anything else — or even if there is. Run annual sweet peas up taut threads of fishing line outside windows for a change of scenery. Drape pillars and posts with long-flowering fragrant climbers. Good choices for this draping include the climbing roses 'Crepuscule', 'Iceberg' and 'New Dawn', as well as some jasmines, including poet's jasmine, Azores jasmine and Arabian jasmine. Each of these jasmines have shrubby tendencies so they will need regular clipping.

Use any of the hanging basket suggestions in the plan as well as peppermint-scented geranium, *Gardenia augusta* 'Radicans' and patio roses. All but the patio roses will tolerate light shade. Stage-manage fragrance by moving plants to accessible and strategic positions — such as near doors and windows — when they are at their most fragrant.

All the plants that are recommended for growing in hanging baskets (except *Gardenia augusta* 'Radicans' and daphne) are suitable for window boxes, along with pinks, stock, sweet alyssum and sweet violet.

If your house has an upper level, consider using climbers in window boxes so foliage and flowers hang down in fragrant tresses.

Chapter 3

The Touching Garden

Luxury of luxuries!
I've been lying on my own thyme lawn.

Edna Walling (1896–1973)

Of all the senses, touch receives the least attention, yet its power to create mood and enchantment in the garden is enormous. The sensations we feel as we move around the garden have an immediate effect on our mood, and leave us with a lasting impression.

If you want a garden that lures you time and time again, add a pleasurable tactile dimension. Use 'touch' as another phial of magic potion with which to cast a spell.

Scent and taste may be a matter of personal preference, but when it comes to our sense of touch, it seems, we are more likely to agree. Some plants have universal appeal — they beg to be touched. High on the list are felty, downy-leafed plants, such as lamb's ear (*Stachys byzantina*), and also peppermint-scented geranium, dusty miller

(*Centaurea cineraria*) and helichrysum (*Helichrysum petiolare*). Each is perfect for edging or, better still, raised beds. Their soft hues of silver, white and lime green make them all the more enticing. Pick a leaf — all these plants have plenty to spare — and wander the garden with it in hand for tactile company. Lamb's ear in particular, brushed against the cheek or under the chin, is wonderful. Its underbelly, just like a lamb's, is especially woolly.

In fact, wherever felty texture is seen in the garden it catches the eye and lures the hand — mossy rocks, the fuzzy flowers of Mexican sage (*Salvia leucantha*) and flannel flower (*Actinotus helianthi*), the downy cheeks of peaches, even the furry seed capsules of wisteria and akebia. The soft tree fern (*Dicksonia antarctica*) has a well-kept secret known only to the connoisseur of touch with its shallow furry nest, as soft and cosy as a kangaroo's pouch, at the top of its trunk.

Fern fronds, too, attract our touch, as do other lacy, intricate textures: threads of fine grasses, tiny-leafed Corsican mint and baby's tears (*Soleirolia soleirolii*). Often their touch is so light that it is hardly a sensation at all — like wispy asparagus tops, the pink plumes of fountain grass (*Pennisetum alopecuroides*) or the petals of a full-blown rose that falls apart in the hand.

But all is not soft and fluffy — nor predictable — in the Touching Garden. We are also attracted to the most stiff and starched of leaves — those of oleaster, holly and *Mahonia*, for instance. In fact, some of the most irresistible plants are those that we know will not please us — plants with spines and thorns. Perversely, the longer and more dangerous the spike, the more it tempts us to test it with a thumb. Similarly, plants with spiky, thistle-like flowers or leaves, such as seaholly and cardoon, add a sense of excitement because of the dangers they suggest. We don't even need to touch them. Bristle-leafed borage and gunnera, even raspy heliotrope, set a mood of anticipation.

Some plants have surfaces that seem so out of context in the garden, we need to touch them to confirm that they are in fact real: waxy tulips and magnolia flowers, the coral-like leaves of silver santolina and the round bumps on the margins of *Aloe vera*, for example. Some fleshy leaves, like those of sedum, plead to be snapped, yet weep tears when we do so.

Dense foliage and flowers urge us to stroke and pat. A hand will always reach out to enjoy tightly clipped topiary or a manicured hedge; if it is fragrant, like rosemary, all the better. The packed flower heads of some plants — hydrangeas, for instance — have a similar magnetism, but in this case we are drawn to pat with open palms and rejoice in the always pleasing springy sensation.

Barks offer a variety of textures — everything from stringy, spongy, rough and fissured to alabaster. Smooth-trunked gum trees provide the latter, most notably lemon-scented gum (*Eucalyptus citriodora*) and snow gum (*Eucalyptus pauciflora*). One of the finest, most irresistible trunks is that of crepe myrtle. Smooth and mottled with tones of apricot and pink, it has the feel of wood weathered by the ocean. Thankfully, it is not modest and throws off its leaves each autumn for all to see.

Some plants reach out for us, like a kiss-curl of akebia from an arch, or the feathery leaves of artemisia that tickle us as we pass. Care must be taken, however, to ensure plants that greet us are friend, not foe: like the thorny tentacles of a rose.

Just for fun, include a few plants that *react* to touch. Impatiens has seed heads that explode at the slightest touch, while the feathery leaves of sensitive plant (*Mimosa pudica*) recoil and snap together.

Consider how your garden feels underfoot. Bricks, pavers, stone, concrete, pebbles and timber decking have their own feel, as do more natural surfaces such as grass, groundcovers and mulches. Each of these is capable of entirely altering the mood of a garden.

One of the most pleasant surfaces to walk on is a soft mattress of needles dropped by pines and casuarinas. This can — quite literally — put a spring in your step. In a large garden it is worth planting a little grove for this sensation alone. A similar effect can be achieved in smaller gardens with a thick layer of bark chips.

There are practical considerations, too, and the most important of all is sureness of foot. Slippery, bumpy surfaces set us on edge and distract our attention from the surroundings — no matter how captivating they may be.

Exploring the garden barefoot can be fun. So why not make a path especially for the purpose: chamomile, thyme, dichondra, Corsican mint and baby's tears are natural choices, and all tolerate light foot traffic. Add a seat along the way, and a smooth water-worn rock that becomes a footrest warmed by the sun.

In fact, using the elements to your advantage is vital to the success of the Touching Garden. Feeling the warmth of the sun while you lie outstretched on grass surely provides one of the garden's most underrated pleasures; yet blinding heat rates as one of the worst. Similarly, a sea breeze on a midsummer's day is a very different experience to a howling gale. Where possible, take charge of the elements. Choose deciduous trees for summer shade and winter sun. Create windbreaks against blustering winds and open doorways to cooling summer breezes.

In planning a Touching Garden, the potential for making use of water should not be overlooked. Falling or spraying water is particularly pleasant, especially in summer. Nearby, the air pops with pleasure, like bubbles in champagne, and charges the skin, making it even more receptive.

As you can see, the sense of touch is far from inert; it is more than just a bystander to the happy antics of the other senses. It even brings its own set of expectations. In a formal setting, for example, it demands fine finishes and smooth textures. In a wilder part of the garden, on the other hand, it expects rustic, even rough-hewn, structures.

Whenever you create a garden, choose its mood or purpose and use touch as your accomplice to make it work. For a restful haven, aim for billowing clouds of downy plants in bunny-rug hues. An outdoor office, however, with laptops and mobile phones, is no place for lullabies, so unleash the garden's power to enliven by combining wide-awake colours with stiff leaves, and out-of-reach spikes and spines.

Too often touch is the cooped-up and neglected caged bird of the senses. Resolve to listen to it. Yield to its whims and desires. Let it frolic. The garden will benefit and so — no doubt — will you.

Plan for a Touching Garden

Lamb's ear and peppermint-scented geranium, with leaves to touch and pick, mark the entry to the Touching Garden. Inside, a spongy, bark-chip path, laid deep, encircles a grassy centre.

To the left is *Camellia sasanqua* with its lower branches removed to make a small tree. In the cooler months the camellia is covered in fine-petalled flowers; collect handfuls of the petals to scatter in float bowls dotted about the garden.

Underneath the *Camellia sasanqua*, baby's tears and maidenhair fern thrive in the shade. A few steps onward is a drinking fountain, with a mossy cushion to kneel on at its base, overhung by

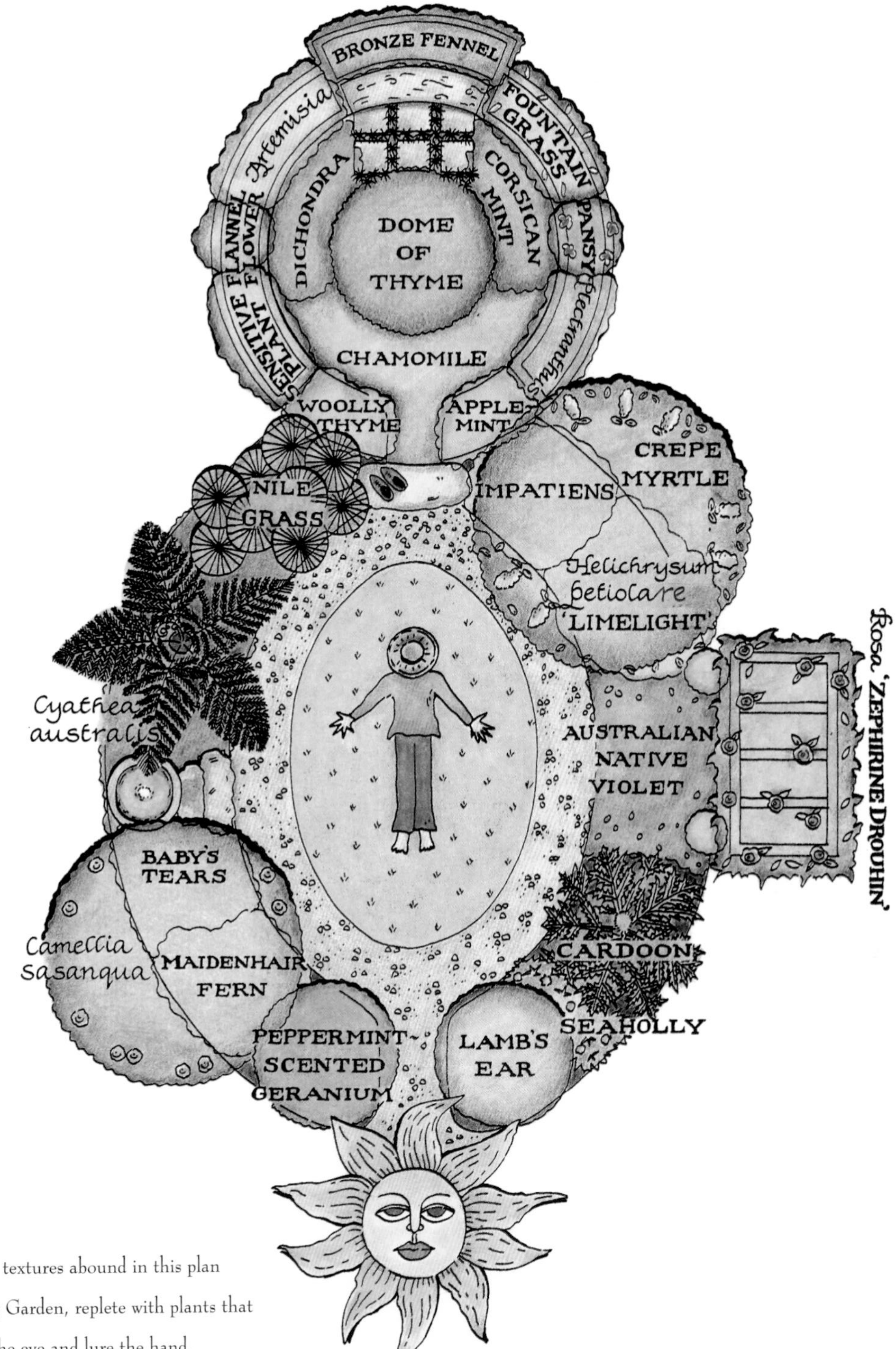

BRONZE FENNEL

FOUNTAIN GRASS

Artemisia

DICHONDRA

CORSICAN MINT

SENSITIVE PLANT FLANNEL FLOWER

PANSY Pelargonium ionidiflora

DOME OF THYME

CHAMOMILE

WOOLLY THYME

APPLE MINT

NILE GRASS

IMPATIENS

CREPE MYRTLE

Helichrysum petiolare 'LIMELIGHT'

Cyathea australis

AUSTRALIAN NATIVE VIOLET

Rosa 'ZEPHIRINE DROUHIN'

BABY'S TEARS

Camellia sasanqua

MAIDENHAIR FERN

CARDOON

PEPPERMINT SCENTED GERANIUM

LAMB'S EAR

SEA HOLLY

Irresistible textures abound in this plan
for a Touching Garden, replete with plants that
catch the eye and lure the hand.

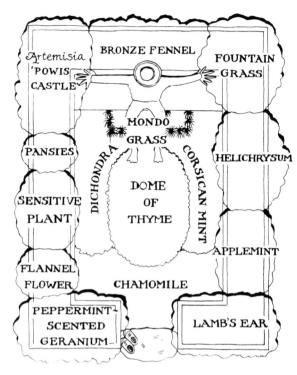

ARTEMISIA 'POWIS CASTLE'

BRONZE FENNEL

FOUNTAIN GRASS

PANSIES

DICHONDRA

MONDO GRASS

CORSICAN MINT

HELICHRYSUM

SENSITIVE PLANT

DOME OF THYME

FLANNEL FLOWER

CHAMOMILE

APPLEMINT

PEPPERMINT SCENTED GERANIUM

LAMB'S EAR

Turn a neglected corner into a small Touching Garden incorporating your most favoured stroke-friendly plants — portions of the larger plan can easily be accommodated in the smallest of spaces.

Cyathea australis; this sun-tolerant, moisture-loving tree fern combines enormous fronds with a white woolly trunk. The silky stems of adjacent Nile grass (*Cyperus papyrus*) are within easy reach of the path, and stand sentinel-like at the entry of a looped Barefoot Garden.

Here, chamomile, dichondra and Corsican mint trail around a dome of thyme — a perfect place to sit and enjoy the barefoot trail up-close. In a raised bed, just within reach, is sensitive plant, along with felty, furry and velvety sensations in petals and leaves courtesy of artemisia, fountain grass, flannel flower, pansies and *Plectranthus argentatus*. Wispy fennel shades a seat that has mondo grass — grown there for you to run your toes through — at its base. As you exit, brush your feet over woolly thyme and fruity-scented applemint.

Further around the pathway, the smooth trunk of crepe myrtle is within reach. Growing beneath is impatiens with its exploding seed pods and gold helichrysum (*Helichrysum petiolare* 'Limelight'). The old climbing Bourbon rose 'Zephirine Drouhin', nearby, covers a timber arbour. Completely without thorns, this rose's deliciously scented carmine-pink flowers provide petals to hold in cupped hands and shower about the garden. In front of the arbour, tightly clipped balls of small-leafed honeysuckle (*Lonicera nitida*) sit in pots on a carpet of Australian native violet.

A garden of intriguing shapes and textures follows as you continue along the pathway. A towering cardoon with jagged leaves and pink-purple thistle-like flowers, and spiny blue seaholly flowers tempt you to touch and test yet again.

Finally, the circumnavigation complete, there is the centre of the garden — that lush swathe of green grass — a perfect place to stretch out with a book or abandon yourself to restful dreams.

A Smaller Touching Garden

The large plan for a Touching Garden is easily trimmed into smaller vignettes. Many gardens, for example, have a neglected corner that can be made into a barefoot trail. Alternatively, convert an existing garden path — one that gets only light or infrequent foot traffic — into a barefoot path.

If you have a large garden bed, carve a path for access through the foliage. Apart from the opportunity this offers to feel leaves brushing against your bare legs, it will make weeding your vegetable patch or picking your strawberry crop easier and more enjoyable. Contain the barefoot path with a border of timber, bricks or tiles. Corsican mint, dichondra and baby's tears are the best choices for shady sections.

If you have an area of uninspiring lawn, consider claiming a portion just for lying on. Choose a mostly sunny spot, with a little summer shade, then sow, plant or turf with the most luxuriant living carpet you can find. To keep this area pristine, be sure to isolate it from the general lawn, by raising the area slightly with a brick-edge surround, perhaps. This will reduce passing foot traffic, act as a barrier to weeds and grass runners from the other part of the lawn, and ensure rapid drying after rain.

Apart from winter green grass, as suggested in the larger plan, consider soft buffalo, Durban grass (also known as sweet smother grass), or non-turf options such as chamomile and thyme.

A Tiny Touching Garden

Some of the tiniest spaces make the best Touching Gardens because the plants are so close, touching them is inevitable. At a nursery, test out as many small plants as possible, especially those that are listed for use in the Barefoot Garden. Tuck a comfortable seat in amongst your favourite luxuriant foliage, then carpet beneath and all around with plant sensations.

For a terrace area, those blessed with practical skills, or practical friends, could build a shallow wooden box in which to grow a low, verdant living mat for under tables and chairs.

Corsican mint and baby's tears will live happily in the shallowest of boxes, and will spill over the edge to cover the box entirely; they will also enjoy the shade that life under tables and chairs can afford.

Water features are surprisingly space-effective, and can usually be achieved on a terrace or even a balcony. Wall fountains are probably the best choice, as they can take up less room than you would expect — many will take up less space than a potted plant. Shop around for a fountain of the ideal dimensions, but also think about other watery options available — shallow terracotta saucers make ideal float bowls for flowers and feet to share on hot summer days.

All plants used in the Barefoot Garden, on the ground and in raised beds, are suitable for growing in pots and window boxes. For shade, maidenhair fern, Australian native violet and peppermint-scented geranium are also suitable.

Utilising all available above-ground space, the best choices for hanging baskets in sun or part-shade are thyme, chamomile, lamb's ear, pansies and applemint.

Why not create a Touching Garden on a wall or fence. Half-baskets and wall-mounted pots look sensational when used en masse, especially when filled with a thematic collection of plants such as scented geraniums, which are easily grown and ideal for sunny spots. And there are dozens to collect. Their range of textures includes stiff, crinkle-cut, soft, felty, ferny and dainty. Their scents include pepper-mint, rose, lemon, lime, orange, apple, nut-meg, spice, coconut, sherbet and musk, to name a few.

Chapter 4

The Tasting Garden

What wond'rous life is this I lead!
Ripe apples drop about my head,
The luscious clusters of the vine,
Upon my mouth do crush their wine;
The nectarine and curious peach,
Into my hands themselves do reach;
Stumbling on melons as I pass,
Insnar'd with flow'rs, I fall on grass.

Andrew Marvell (1621–1678), *The Garden*

Why not have a garden just for tasting. Not for dinner, jams or chutneys, but just for tasting. Right there, on the spot, as you wander the garden, perhaps with a friend.

In the Tasting Garden of our dreams, flowers, vegetables, herbs and fruits interweave, and finding and collecting things to eat is part of the fun. The problem becomes not where to look, but rather, where to look first. On hands and knees we tickle beneath foliage to find ripe strawberries, stretch across herbs to snap off a snowpea, stand on tiptoe to pick a bunch of grapes, then climb a ladder into the boughs of an apple or mulberry tree to collect the juiciest fruit of the day.

With a basket lined with vine leaves, scissors in hand, we collect the makings of a feast: fruits, crisp salad greens, a few carrots cool from the earth, a sprinkling of nuts, radishes, cucumber, and a single thread of chives. We toss in a lemon or lime, and a handful of edible flowers: sweet violets, daylilies, little blue borage stars, and nasturtiums in shades of saffron, ginger, ruby and cinnamon.

Then, under the shade of a pergola, we create a plate of splendour. We might mix sweet with savoury, and crisp with velvety, sit fruit and nuts atop salad greens. Toss or compose. Then use flowers as colourful jewels scattered on top. With fresh, perfect ingredients little effort is required. This is hand-to-mouth living at its best, using food that never needs to see the drudgery or dreariness of the inside of a kitchen.

If you have a garden with plenty of sun, the Tasting Garden is yours for the making. Even the smallest garden is suitable, with the right choice and

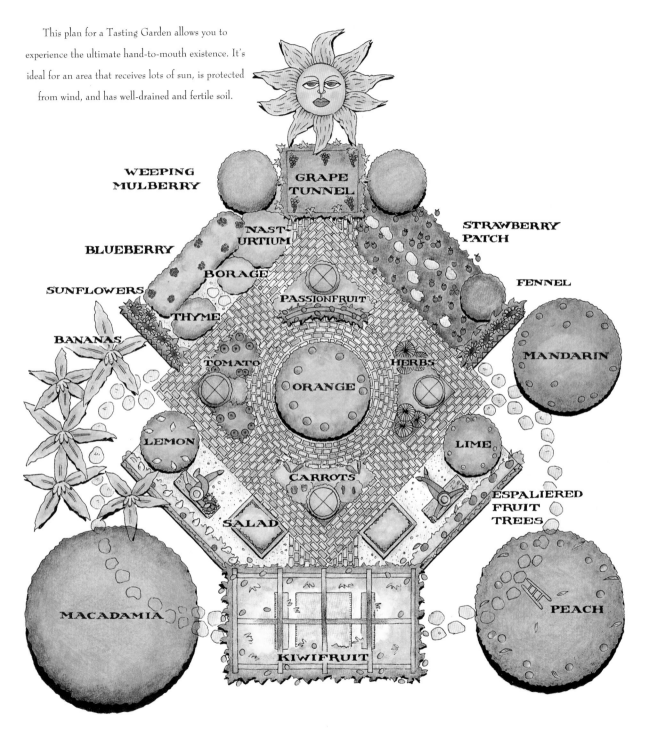

This plan for a Tasting Garden allows you to experience the ultimate hand-to-mouth existence. It's ideal for an area that receives lots of sun, is protected from wind, and has well-drained and fertile soil.

WEEPING MULBERRY

GRAPE TUNNEL

STRAWBERRY PATCH

NASTURTIUM

BLUEBERRY

BORAGE

FENNEL

SUNFLOWERS

PASSIONFRUIT

THYME

MANDARIN

BANANAS

TOMATO

HERBS

ORANGE

LEMON

LIME

CARROTS

ESPALIERED FRUIT TREES

SALAD

MACADAMIA

KIWIFRUIT

PEACH

use of plants. And there are plenty of plants from which to choose. In fact, the sheer abundance of foods available for growing is incredible, and it's getting bigger. There are all the newcomers — varieties that love the climates their parents pooh-poohed, trees that combine two fruits (such as plums and apricots) on a single trunk, and dwarf versions of fruit trees, small enough for the tiniest garden. And then there are the old species and varieties: tasty, long-forgotten fruits waiting to be rediscovered, heirloom vegetables you've never dreamed of, and ancient foods from far-flung lands.

One of the most seductive things about the Tasting Garden is the opportunity it offers to experience tastes that money simply cannot buy. Some of the tastiest foods are never available in the shops because they do not transport or last well. Growing them yourself may be the only way to experience their exquisite qualities and nuances.

Almost without exception, the tastiest plants want the same thing — a sun-drenched place, protected from wind, with well-drained, fertile soil. These factors are basic to the Tasting Garden — its success hinges on them.

It is also important to search out the plants that thrive in your climate, especially when growing the larger, more permanent residents of the tasting garden — the fruit and nut trees. Research is the key. Speak to as many people in local clubs, societies, government departments, nurseries and organisations as you can. Visit gardens to see what fruit and nut trees other people are growing locally.

Make delectability of taste your top priority. Some plants with really delicious-sounding names are actually cooking or non-fruiting ornamental varieties so, clearly, these are not for the Tasting Garden; nor are the increasing numbers of genuinely edible plants, marketed for their taste, which may well fail to live up to expectations. Always do a taste test if you can.

With your list of 'thrivers' in hand, the next challenge is to cram every one of your favourite fruits and nuts into the allotted space and still leave room for vegetables, herbs and flowers. Dwarf varieties may be available, for example. These are the real thing in miniature — the same fruit on a small plant. And some are very small indeed. Some varieties of dwarf apples can grow less than 1 metre (3 ft) high and produce up to 20 fruit at a time. Some are bred to grow in a column-like way to preserve ground space.

Using plants that grow up, rather than out, is the key to getting the most from your space. Some fruits, such as passionfruit, grapes and kiwifruit need little encouragement. With a little support, they can be used to cascade over fences, scale walls, and climb pergolas. Tripods, pillars, arches and picket fences make great supports for peas, beans, tomatoes and cucumbers, tossing them in the air like a juggling act. But how can we squeeze full-scale fruit trees into a small space?

Necessity has been the mother of many beautiful inventions in the Tasting Garden, and espalier is one. Espalier combines training plants along wires with diligent pruning. It shoehorns a spreading plant into the smallest possible ground space, making it possible to grow four or five fruit trees in an area no bigger than 5 metres (15 ft) long and 30 cm (12 in) wide. You can train plants against an existing fence or wall, or erect poles and wires to make garden dividers.

One of the most popular espalier patterns is to have branches outstretched at perfect right angles to a straight trunk. But almost anything is possible. Pick a style to suit your purpose. For example, espalier a pear tree against the walls of your house to frame the windows and doors with its branches.

Apples and pears are the easiest and most popular fruit trees to train as espaliers. Oranges, lemons, figs, peaches, almonds, apricots, nectarines, red currants, white currants and plums are also worth trying for imaginative espalier.

Diligence and determination are the key skills in creating espaliers. As food and garden writer Richard Beckett suggests: 'Think of it as a giant bonsai or a slow wrestle with an alligator.' But the result is well worth the effort, especially if you have a small garden, because it makes all sorts of clever (and beautiful) space-saving ideas possible. With an underlying frame, fruit and nut trees can be encouraged to form arches, arbours and pergolas. Plain paths can be transformed into fruiting tunnels by planting an avenue of young trees and interlacing their supple stems overhead. The fruit in such tunnels dangles into our hands, but well out of the reach of birds in search of a fruity feast.

Standards are also worth considering if you have training and pruning in mind. These plants with round heads of foliage on clean trunks can often be purchased ready-trained; all you need to do is to keep them in check. Gooseberries, red and white currants, many citrus fruits and grafted weeping mulberries make elegant standards.

If you have room for a full-sized fruit tree, consider 'duo' or 'trio' planting. This space-saving concept is the brainchild of fruit-tree specialist Dawn Fleming of Fleming's Nurseries in Victoria. Two or three fruit trees are planted in the same hole, about 15 cm (6 in) apart. The result is a variety of different tastes over a longer period, and all in the space required for a single tree.

Given plenty of water early in life, duos and trios grow happily together, and may even produce more fruit through cross-pollination (when two cultivars of the same tree, such as 'Granny Smith' and 'Jonathon' apples, are planted nearby and bees pick up pollen from one and take it to the other). Apples, pears, plums, almonds and cherries have all been used successfully in 'duo' plantings, as have apricots, peaches and nectarines.

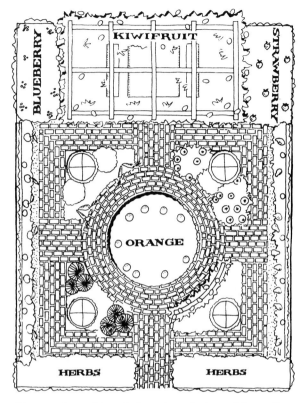

The inner diamond from the large plan is the focus of this smaller Tasting Garden. Make the most of above-ground space — use tripods, arches, maypoles, tepees and poles, as well as walls and fences, to support a feast of fruit and vegetables.

Once the taller things are out of the way, the remaining space is carpeted with smaller-growing plants. Position perennial herbs according to height, how much you'll use them and how often they'll need harvesting. Strawberries, laden with juicy crops for months on end, need a spot right next to a path, whereas asparagus, which is harvested for a shorter time, can be planted a little further away.

Next, colour-in the gaps with annuals for an ever-changing feast. You will want some well-known plants, with their incomparable, fresh-picked flavour — carrots and explode-in-your-mouth cherry tomatoes in particular. But be sure to experiment. Plant a patch of freesias, for example, to provide that secret sip of honey you'll find at the base of each flower.

Finally, don't forget the bees. A touch of the bee's magic wand ensures blossoms are transformed, fairy god-mother-like, into incredibly delectable morsels. Salvia and catmint (*Nepeta* x *faassenii*) attract bees from miles around, and they're a good filler for hard-to-reach spaces. Borage and thyme, two more bee favourites, have edible flowers and leaves, respectively, making them just right for planting next to paths.

More than any other, a Tasting Garden should be an evolution — an ongoing search for the pick of your region's crop. Given that many a fruit and nut tree outlives its planter, you will be providing not just for yourself but for those who follow. Here's to a flavoursome future.

Plan for a Tasting Garden

A grape tunnel, with a pair of weeping mulberries on either side of it, leads into the Tasting Garden. Inside, the air is rich with the sweet scent of fruit. Strong symmetry and bold patterning of garden beds, paths and paving bring order to the teeming jungle of food plants.

The focus of this garden is a central diamond where four island beds surround an orange tree.

A tripod in the corner of each island bed supports cucumbers, climbing beans, green peas, snow-peas and other climbing vegetables according to the season. In the garden nearest the entry, a passionfruit-clad trellis ensures the garden is not seen in a single glance, adding mystery and an enticement to explore. This bed also contains asparagus. The other island beds contain tomatoes and basil; carrots, capsicums (sweet peppers) and chillies (chili peppers); and a selection of favourite herbs.

Flanking the sides of the central diamond are four rectangular areas. The beds closest to the entrance offer an instant feast of strawberries and blueberries. Also planted here are fennel and thyme, along with nasturtiums and borage for a supply of edible flowers. Looking down on this scene, sunflowers supported by picket fences are grown for their seeds.

The two remaining rectangular sections have paved areas, fruit trees and salad greens. Up to eight fruit trees can be squeezed into these two spaces. Six of them — three apples, two pears and a nashi fruit — are espaliered on wires. They provide a beautiful backdrop for these areas and the fruit is easily picked from bench-seats, as are the lemons and limes that grow in large tubs.

The salad greens — include a good variety of favourites you'll use often, such as lettuce, rocket, spring onions (scallions) and radish — can be grown in the ground, but raised benches make them even more accessible and appealing.

These benches are near the eating area of the Tasting Garden — a large table under the shade of a vine-draped pergola at which you can sample the rewards of this paradise for taste-buds. The vine above and around is kiwifruit, a delicious and nutritious native of China which requires both male and female plants to be grown together to ensure fruiting; a male and two females are planted here.

Paths lead off the main Tasting Garden, meander beneath larger fruit and nut trees and then return. These tasting tours include a walk through a banana grove underplanted with mint, a chance to collect macadamia nuts and mandarins, and a journey up a ladder into rambling a peach tree.

Most of the smaller plants, herbs, vegetables and flowering plants used in this plan can be grown in a wide range of climates. The fruit and nut trees, however, are suited to humid, warm temperate areas. If your garden is in a different climate zone, selecting substitutions is an easy matter, with the right advice. For information on the best species and varieties of trees and plants to grow in your area, contact local fruit growers and the nearest office of the department of agriculture.

Finally, be sure to take an organic path to the Tasting Garden. Remember that manures, compost, mulch and natural pest control ensure the safest and the tastiest bounty.

A Smaller Tasting Garden

Use the inner diamond of the large plan as a courtyard outside your front or back door, and espalier fruit trees against sunny fences and walls. Use tripods, arches, maypoles, tepees and poles to support climbing vegetables and fruits, planting low-growing food plants such as lettuce, carrots, asparagus and strawberries around them.

If you have a straight path in full sun, consider turning it into a fruiting tunnel, with apples, pears, grapes, scarlet runner beans or kiwifruit. Or plant an avenue of espaliered fruit trees either side for a formal effect. If the path is short, make an archway. For an open effect, create hedges of blueberries, raspberries and hazelnuts on either side.

Resist the temptation to fill the entire area with plants. Leave space for a table and chairs so that you have somewhere to sit and savour the smells, sights and tastes of this small but sumptuous garden oasis. If space is tight, instead of a pergola, consider an edible arbour using espaliered fruit trees on three sides with stems interlaced to enclose it overhead.

And, remember, the smaller the garden, the more important it is to grow the tastes you most enjoy, so be selective. Keep records of the annual vegetables you plant, including the variety. Collect the seeds of the tastiest crops so you can enjoy them again next year.

A Tiny Tasting Garden

Take advantage of all sunny walls, fences, even balcony railings, if room is severely limited. Drape them in any of the climbers mentioned as suitable for the Smaller Tasting Garden's fruiting tunnel, or espalier fruit or nut trees against them. Even walls of balconies can be used — with plants in pots. In cool climates, fruit and nut trees may appreciate the warmth of a brick wall, but in warmer conditions, the heat may roast the leaves, so provide a trellis — erect it about 20 cm (8 in) away from the wall.

A surprising number of edible plants live happily in pots, including dwarf fruit trees, blueberries and strawberries; most are also suitable for espalier. Some of the best vegetables which will grow in pots are lettuce, tomatoes, peas, beans and chillies (chili peppers). Climbers such as snowpeas grown on tripods look great in pairs either side of a doorway.

Among the best tasting plants for hanging baskets and window boxes are herbs, strawberries, lettuce, sweet violets, nasturtiums and compact varieties of tomatoes.

The salad bench in the large plan is a tasty idea for a balcony or small courtyard. Along with salad plants, include strawberries, chillies, cherry tomatoes and carrots. Experiment with fragrance and edible flowers and foliage such as bronze fennel and purple-leafed basil. Make sumptuous three-dimensional tapestries, then devour them.

Chapter 5

The Night Garden

Be still my soul. Consider
The flowers and the stars.
Among these sleeping fragrances,
Sleep now your cares.

Gerald Bullett (1894–1958)

We usually think of the garden as a place for daytime pleasure but, with careful planning, it can be just as enjoyable by night. As the light wanes and one sense fades, others become stronger. Fragrance, sound and even texture become important. This makes the night garden a special sensory garden — one where all the senses should conspire to create a garden that will soothe and delight when the sun goes down.

Fragrance is one of the great joys of the night garden, and the quality of fragrant sensations is somewhat different in darkness. As dusk creeps in, scent around the garden undergoes a change. Some perfumes that were strong by day fade away; others pour out into the darkness, almost as if to take their place; others still become stronger or change quality and nuance.

Every night garden needs the fragrance of night flowers — those which bloom after nightfall — and it's fun to see them come to life. Some you can set your watch by. And, when they finally 'wake and utter [their] fragrance in a garden sleeping' as Edna St Vincent Millay described it, theirs are the richest and most haunting.

Among the best night-opening flowers are the lemon-scented blooms of evening primrose (*Oenothera biennis*), clove-scented climbing moonflower (*Ipomoea alba*), night-scented stock (*Matthiola bicornis*), sweet white tobacco (*Nicotiana alata*), sweet rocket (*Hesperis matronalis*) and the vanilla-scented postage stamp plant (*Schizopetalon walkeri*). Most of these are annuals to be planted each spring.

Another annual plant that may surprise you with its perfume is the petunia. Some have a delicious vanilla fragrance at night-time but, unfortunately, in the quest for colour and 'bigger and better' flowers, this quality has been bred out of most strains. Consequently, finding them is a bit of a gamble. White and purple-toned flowerers are most likely to retain this perfume quality.

You may find that a few of the annual night-fragrant plants are not much to look at — night-scented stock, for instance — but most are modest in size and easy to disguise among other plants. Tuck them in with long-lived plants, ones that are fragrant day and night, such as daphne, heliotrope, jasmine, honeysuckle, osmanthus, stock (*Matthiola incana*) and heavenly tuberose (*Polianthes tuberosa*).

With a little more space you can include larger plants. The night-scented jessamines (*Cestrum nocturnum* and *C. parqui*) are meek and unassuming shrubs in the daylight, but by late evening their exotic sweet-spicy perfume fills the air. Frangipani, with its own bewitching fragrance, is another essential; the paddle-shaped leaves and uniform branch patterns create a dramatic silhouette, and it lays a carpet of luminous flowers at its feet. Night-time demands bold effects, and angel's trumpet (*Brugmansia suaveolens*) provides them with its deliciously scented trumpet-shaped flowers that hang down like huge designer lanterns. The cream-flowering form is the most glowing.

It may seem a paradox, but colour choice is all-important in the night garden. Daylight's bright colours and patterns become mere shadows in the moonlight. Taking their place is silver and white, with a dash of lime. These are night-time's unrivalled jewels. Whether of flower or foliage, the night light makes these colours magical. Rather than losing their hue, they shimmer.

Nowhere has this effect been more admired than at Sissinghurst in Kent, in the UK, in Vita Sackville-West's 'White Garden'. There, a walled garden filled with grey and silver leaves and white flowers was designed to be lovely in the dusk. One half of the garden is devoted to an intricate arrangement of sixteen geometric garden beds, each edged with box (*Buxus*) and filled with a different variety of white-flowered plant.

White flowers are particularly effective after dark. Sprinkled about the garden they turn night's dark cloak into a fairyland. The best white flowers for evening are not necessarily the showiest. A perfect bloom is wasted if its finer points cannot be fully appreciated. Shape and quantity — not quality — are most important. For masses of continuous white flowers, sweet alyssum is hard to beat. After nightfall each little mound becomes a galaxy of flowers. It has the added virtue of fragrance, too.

Aim for a variety of flower shapes and sizes. Abelia, *Eriostemon myoporoides* and lemon-scented tea tree (*Leptospermum petersonii*) cover themselves in stars. Camellia, clematis, roses and marguerite daisies turn on larger party lights. Others luminesce in all sorts of interesting shapes, from buddleia's arching cones and white *Kniphofia*'s blazing torches to wisteria's chandeliers. Gaura, often called the butterfly plant, seems even more like hovering butterflies by night as its thin stalks disappear into the darkness.

For radiant foliage, dusty miller (*Centaurea cineraria*) and silver santolina are amongst the closest to white. Yet these plants could hardly be more different in texture. Dusty miller is felty, and intensely white, while santolina has the colour and texture of dried coral. Along paths at night, both make wonderful beacons to guide the wanderer. Clipped tightly into a low hedge, santolina gives paths a particularly luxuriant silver lining.

The night garden needs plenty of these silver highlights or it will be cast in darkness. Some of the best plants to grow in low mounds are silver helichrysum (*Helichrysum petiolare*), *Artemisia* 'Powis Castle', lamb's ear (*Stachys byzantina*) and silver

This Night Garden provides a glow-in-the-dark effect and fragrance with night-opening flowers such as evening primrose, moonflower and sweet rocket.

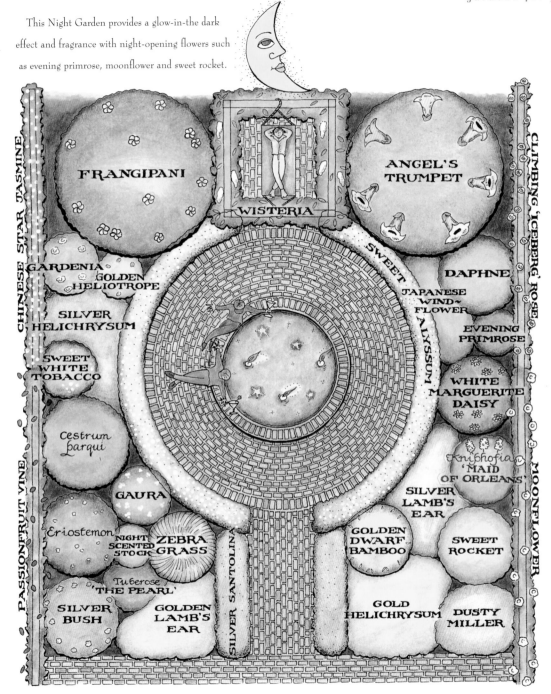

CHINESE STAR JASMINE

PASSIONFRUIT VINE

CLIMBING 'ICEBERG' ROSE

MOONFLOWER

FRANGIPANI

WISTERIA

ANGEL'S TRUMPET

GARDENIA

GOLDEN HELIOTROPE

SILVER HELICHRYSUM

SWEET WHITE TOBACCO

Cestrum parqui

GAURA

Eriostemon

NIGHT SCENTED STOCK

ZEBRA GRASS

Tuberose 'THE PEARL'

SILVER BUSH

GOLDEN LAMB'S EAR

SILVER SANTOLINA

SWEET ALYSSUM

DAPHNE

JAPANESE WIND~FLOWER

EVENING PRIMROSE

WHITE MARGUERITE DAISY

Kniphofia 'MAID OF ORLEANS'

SILVER LAMB'S EAR

GOLDEN DWARF BAMBOO

SWEET ROCKET

GOLD HELICHRYSUM

DUSTY MILLER

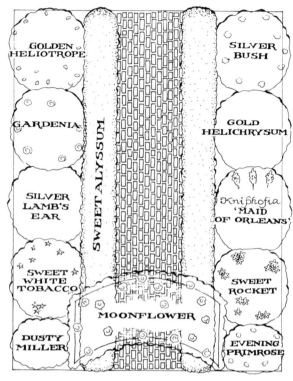

Moonflower drapes an arch to create luminescent drama in this
fragrant and glowing smaller Night Garden.

bush (*Convolvulus cneorum*). Helichrysum's silver-green cultivar 'Limelight', living up to its name, is one of the most glowing of all plants by night.

Consider white and silver in all its forms. Statuary, fences and white-barked eucalypts like lemon-scented gum (*Eucalyptus citriodora*) can act as signposts along a country driveway at night. On a small scale, experiment with the luminous flecks in the variegated leaves of lamium, applemint and ivy.

'Pool rhymes with cool,' wrote Vita Sackville-West, 'and that is what a pool ought to be, a place to sit by on a summer evening, watching the reflections in the water, and the swallows swooping after the insects.' In medieval Japan pools of water

were used in moon gardens to mirror the night sky. Polished chrome gives this idea a contemporary twist. A sleek metal sheet makes a starry table for night dining; a shiny ball on a plinth becomes a divine centrepiece for a night garden; and shiny leaves reflect the night light in a more earthly way. Passionfruit, with its glossy leaves, white flowers and delicious fruit, is a star performer on a trellis in the night garden.

Speaking of performances, night music is also invaluable. Some of the best sounds are provided by splashing water, with a rustling grassy-leafed accompaniment such as bamboo, lemon grass and zebra grass (*Miscanthus sinensis* 'Zebrinus'). Animals can also play a part: add a dovecote for the gentle cooing of fantail doves or a gleaming pond which may attract a baritone frog.

An ideal location for a night garden is near an outdoor living area — a place where you can dine alfresco or simply relax at the end of the day. Use glow-in-the-dark plants in pots, and in the surrounding garden too. Artificial light will work to enhance the magic, as will subtle lighting around the table from candles, flares or a soft uplighter on a nearby wall. In the garden itself, hide the light source from view and use beams as spotlights, backlights or 'washes'. Create a vista, beautiful by day, that really sparkles at night.

By all means consider a second night garden, too — one tucked further away from the house. Here you will be able to surround yourself with the night and become a part of it — you can eavesdrop on its sounds, and wallow in its scents and sights. With a spot to lie down you can enjoy the best show in town. And while the heavens provide plenty of interest to the naked eye, they become more magnificent through binoculars or a small telescope.

A place like this may become your favourite hideaway — somewhere to seek rest and rejuvenation after a hard day's work.

Plan for a Night Garden

The Night Garden has been designed to provide a sweeping view from an adjoining outdoor living area. From here, mounds of silver and gold are spotlit by the moon and outdoor lighting. Luminous white flowers in various shapes and sizes are dotted throughout. The air is rich with scent, especially when the night-bloomers begin to pour their fragrance into the air.

A path, edged in clipped silver santolina, entices you to enter. On one side of the garden fragrance is a heady mix of Tuberose 'The Pearl', night-scented stock, golden heliotrope, sweet white tobacco, Cestrum parqui and gardenia. Many of these, along with Eriostemon and gaura, have white or lime-coloured flowers. Silver bush, silver helichrysum and golden lamb's ear (Stachys byzantina 'Primrose Heron') glow in the dark, and passionfruit vine and Chinese star jasmine (Trachelospermum jasminoides) cover a fence or trellis.

On the other side of the garden, on another trellis, the climbing 'Iceberg' rose and moonflower offer fragrant white flowers. In the garden below are glowing mounds of dusty miller, silver lamb's ear and gold helichrysum. Apart from moonflower, fragrance also comes from some sweet rocket, evening primrose and daphne; and more white in flowers is provided by Japanese windflower, Kniphofia 'Maid of Orleans' and, finally, marguerite daisy.

In the central area of the garden the path sweeps around a small pool with a low 'sitting wall' from which you can happily watch the reflections of the moon and stars. On special occasions scented candles can be floated on the pond's watery surface. Sweet alyssum edges this part of the garden and, nearby, zebra grass and the golden dwarf bamboo rustle their reedy leaves in the night-time breezes.

The largest plants in the Night Garden are frangipani and angel's trumpet. Their interesting forms frame a simple pergola, with a hammock slung beneath. The pergola itself is clothed in Wisteria floribunda 'Alba', with its impossibly long racemes, catching the light and swaying in the breeze. It is carefully trained and pruned along the four beams of the pergola, leaving the centre open to the heavens above.

Lying in the gently swinging hammock, an outdoor planetarium is revealed through a wisteria 'window'. The scents of frangipani and angel's trumpet mingle — exotic, sweet and fruity. Looking up at the stars, life's complexities fade away. There is just us and the universe, with nothing in between.

A Smaller Night Garden

With so many small-growing plants, trimming the large plan to fit your space should not be difficult. Give preference to plants with more than one night-worthy feature. For example, choose silver bush for silver leaves and white flowers; heliotrope, sweet alyssum and gardenia for white flowers and fragrance by day and night; and moonflower and sweet rocket for night blooms and fragrance.

Plant a night garden where it can serve a practical

purpose, too. Either side of a path is a good idea, especially if it is used by visitors who are unfamiliar with the garden.

Remember, gardens in shade or part-shade during the day may also be shaded from the moon at night. If this is the case, you will need to add artificial light, or lamps, for plants to glow. From the plan, the best plants for shaded positions are daphne, gardenia, golden heliotrope, Japanese windflower, white forget-me-not and both silver and gold forms of helichrysum.

A Tiny Night Garden

Even the smallest space can become a Night Garden. At close range it is easier to enjoy the unique antics of night-blooming plants, along with the fascinating night moths they will attract. Almost all of the plants in the plan are suitable for pots. Frangipani and angel's trumpet can be grown in large tubs but they do need space.

Along with other fragrant pots of heliotrope, gardenia and tuberose, these make a fine starting point for a Night Garden. Next, add plants that perform 'tricks'. Any of the annual plants that magically open their blooms at night, including moonflower, can be sown directly into pots. Grow as many as you can. Perhaps you could try to arrange them like a 'Watch of Flora' — an obsession of the great Swedish botanist Carl Linnaeus — in which blooms open in sequence hour by hour. Other plants that open and close at reasonably predictable times during the day and evening include daylily, *Portulaca grandiflora*, four o'clock plant (*Mirabilis jalapa*), Iceland poppy and Californian poppy.

In cool climates, for further novelty, plant the beautiful perennial burning bush (*Dictamnus albus*), which has flower heads on long spires covered in a volatile lemon-scented oil. When ignited with a match on a still summer night they burn like incense. Nottingham catchfly (*Silene nutans*), some say, scatters white stars when it opens.

It has also been said, mainly in books written by enthusiastic gardeners long departed, that evening primrose emits a 'mysterious phosphorescent light', and that it pops open with a 'silver burst of sound'. Most modern plant-loving writers are yet to witness this amazing phenomenon, however there are quite a number of species of evening primrose (*Oenothera*) … perhaps it's just a matter of finding the right one.

If it proves elusive, more silver mounds and night-time sounds may soothe our sorrow.

Living Pleasure Gardens

FRUITING HEDGE

Clematis aristata

GRASS TREE   RED SALVIA

BUDDLEIA

KANGAROO PAW

BUTTERFLY FLOWER

Grevillea 'ROBYN GORDON'

BLACKTHORN

BLUE BOG SALVIA

Grevillea 'POORINDA ROYAL MANTLE'

RED HOT POKER

MOONFLOWER

Correa alba

IMPATIENS

LILLY PILLY

Indigofera australis

Lantana montevidensis

SWEET VIOLET

HOUSE

Chapter 6

The Bird Garden

There is a smiling summer here,
which causes birds to sing.

Emily Dickinson (1830–1886)

When it comes to bringing colour, life and song to a garden, birds are the unrivalled champions, yet we often take them for granted, or fail to take the time to appreciate their presence. On a warm sunny day when the birds wing in to play in the trees and sing songs to each other, pull up a seat and take in the show.

If you are lucky they may stage a backyard drama of chases, spills and thrills, or perhaps even perform circus acts on a grevillea trapeze. Mostly they offer tunes and gentle company, wearing some of the most vivid and startling costumes the animal kingdom has to offer.

Anyone who dreams of a garden filled with birds will be pleased to know that the needs of these creatures are nowhere near as diverse as the entertainment they provide. Some needs, such as water, are universal. And even with food there is a recipe for success — a smorgasbord of nectar, seeds, fruit and insects will provide something to please every one of them.

The plant component of this feast — the nectar, seeds and fruit — should be chosen with a preference for native plants. Birds and plants will usually have evolved together, so their relationships are often fascinating and complex tales of inter-dependence. By planting a backbone of native species, you will create a garden that is tailor-made to your region's birdlife.

There is no harm in using exotic plants, as long as they support rather than dominate the main scheme. Ask the people at your local native plant society or nursery which plants provide bird foods in the most copious quantities, with the widest seasonal spread. Search out native bird societies too, where members may be able to tell you which are the most endangered bird species in your area and suggest plants to aid their survival.

The key to providing the insect component of the bird's diet is an organic, no-poisons approach to gardening; as any good organic gardener knows, birds are invaluable for keeping garden pests under control. Some birds feed entirely on insects, eating thousands every week, while many others use them as a supplement along with other foods, or to feed their young. Wherever insects gather en masse, birds are rarely far away. Generally speaking, the plants most likely to attract insects in their droves have dense clusters of nectar-rich flowers. Mulch and leaf litter also ensure a good supply of insects.

The layout of the garden plays an important part in the enticement of birds. A design that mimics a forest and a clearing is ideal. Like many wild things, birds feel most comfortable on the edges of forests: this is where they tend to feed and nest, and where you are most likely to see them in the wild. Creating a backyard version of this scene encourages birds to linger, and perhaps even to take up residence. This may sound like a tall order in an average-sized suburban backyard, but it is in fact surprisingly easy to achieve.

The clearing, for example, may be a simple patch of lawn, or a meadow, in the centre of the garden. Surround this area with tufting grasses and low shrubs, building up to a dense understorey of thick shrubs, the denser, thornier and more prickly the better. Birds delight in intricate branches, and no wonder, as these are supermarkets of variety and opportunity, offering everything from insects and nesting materials to safe nesting sites away from predators. Dense shrubs that provide food as well are the best of all. Many grevillea species, for example, are prickly and drip with nectar, making them the most bird-attracting of all plants.

Most gardens will have room for only three or four small trees at most; this is hardly a forest, but the birds won't quibble. Just one tree can provide so many things a bird needs: insects, good vantage points, and a safe place to feast and make nests. Every established tree is an asset; if your garden does not have any, plant a fast-grower.

All birds need cool water for drinking and bathing, so tuck birdbaths and water-filled dishes into shady areas where the 'clearing' and 'forest' meet. Shallow water, where birds can walk right in, is always appreciated; many so-called 'birdbaths' are too deep, and birds use them only for drinking. Even ponds and pools should include a shallow lip. As Edna Walling observed, 'Deep water is terrifying to short-legged feathered folk.'

Remember, too, wherever water is placed near ground level, be sure to provide a quick get-away route: a prickly shrub is a bird's best escape hatch when a cat turns up.

The garden described so far will have plenty of nesting sites: within clumps of grasses, inside prickly shrubs, in the dense understorey and in the forks of high tree branches. But not all birds will be satisfied; some of the most interesting — kookaburras, rosellas, nightjars, owls and countless others — need something more, and that something is a simple hollow tree.

If birds living in urban settings could get together and reminisce about the good old days, dead trees would surely dominate the conversation. The numbers of more than a few species of birds are declining due to a lack of hollow trees in which to nest. If you have a dead tree, or one with dying branches, cover it with a climber if you must, but treasure it for the birds.

If you don't have a dead tree, hollow logs are the next best thing. Anyone who can hammer a nail is capable of making a nesting box from a hollow log. Cut it to about 30 cm (12 in) long. It will be used in an upright position, so give it a roof and a floor by nailing boards to the top and bottom. Allow an overhang on the roof for protection from rain. Drill a hole towards the top of the log. The size of the hole will largely determine the species of bird that will call the log home; between 2 cm (1 in) and 18 cm (7 in) is best. Leave plenty of room between the floor and entrance hole because the birds need a deep cavity to build up the nest with leaves and twigs. A small hole in the base provides drainage in case the rain gets in. Rough construction should ensure plenty of spaces for ventilation. If not, add several small holes around the top. If you have trouble finding hollow logs, chop four barked sides from a log and nail them together.

When installing a nesting box on a pole, make sure it's cat-proof. Metal makes a good base or, if you are using timber, nail a band of metal sheet at least 45 cm (1½ ft) wide around it. A metal sheet can also be used to keep cats out of trees.

Incidentally, when wiring a nesting box into a tree, use small thin strips of timber between the tree and the wire to lessen the likelihood of inadvertent ringbarking. Position the bird-nesting box so it is protected from hot sun and strong winds.

Different birds will prefer different homes: some like a hollow log, others hollow gourds or open-sided shelves; birds have even been known to set up home in an old kettle placed amongst the twigs at the base of a dense shrub. Research has shown that birds are most likely to nest in areas where there is a choice of nesting

sites, so increase your chances by providing as many nesting spots and birdhouses as you can.

During nest-building time in spring you may like to leave useful bits and pieces in the open, and watch them disappear. String, feathers, wool, old hessian bags and pieces of bark are favourites. Mud and cobwebs are helpful too. Have a pile of twiggy prunings and an open compost heap for an extra supply of bite-sized insects for tiny beaks.

The final step in creating a bird sanctuary is to 'fly the boundaries' of your fences and involve neighbouring properties too. Once the neighbours see the fun and action at your place, they shouldn't need much convincing.

Plan for a Bird Garden

The centre of the Bird Garden is a keyhole-shaped area of lawn. A circular seat in the middle allows you to follow the action as it happens. It also doubles as a low table with a hole for a market umbrella on hot sunny days. From this seat, looking around in a clockwise direction, the garden begins with a clump of sunflowers. Sown each spring, they are left to set seed for the birds. Also dropping seeds onto the grass nearby is kangaroo grass (*Themeda australis*) with its oat-like purple-brown heads. The weeping bottlebrush (*Callistemon viminalis*) behind provides shelter and attracts nectar-feeders to its bright red flowers almost all year long. Under its cover, a shallow bird-

This plan for a Bird Garden provides everything a bird could possibly want: water, nectar, seeds, fruit, insects, shelter and adventure.

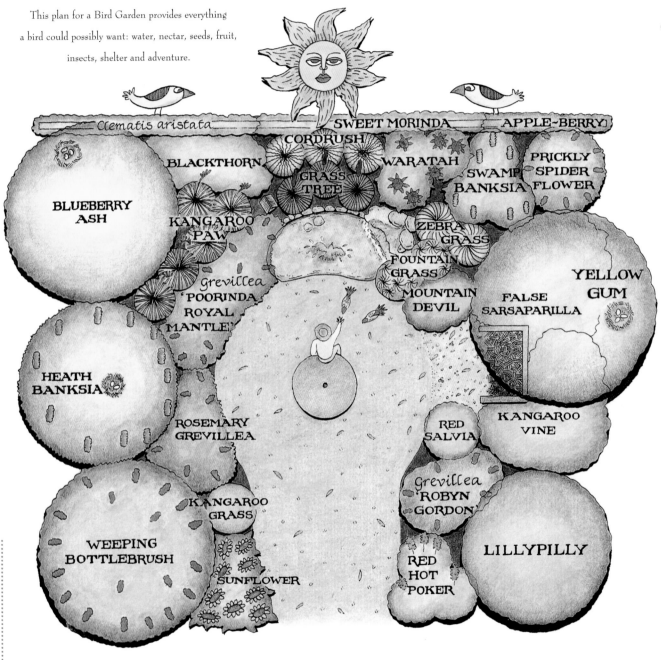

Clematis aristata — SWEET MORINDA — APPLE-BERRY

CORDRUSH

BLACKTHORN

WARATAH

PRICKLY SPIDER FLOWER

SWAMP BANKSIA

GRASS TREE

BLUEBERRY ASH

KANGAROO PAW

ZEBRA GRASS

YELLOW GUM

Grevillea 'POORINDA ROYAL MANTLE'

FOUNTAIN GRASS

MOUNTAIN DEVIL

FALSE SARSAPARILLA

HEATH BANKSIA

ROSEMARY GREVILLEA

RED SALVIA

KANGAROO VINE

Grevillea 'ROBYN GORDON'

KANGAROO GRASS

LILLYPILLY

WEEPING BOTTLEBRUSH

SUNFLOWER

RED HOT POKER

bath is surrounded by the prickly needle-like leaves and nectar-rich flowers of rosemary grevillea (*Grevillea rosmarinifolia*). Neighbouring *Grevillea* 'Poorinda Royal Mantle' is a groundcover with shelter, nesting sites and nectar-filled flowers that are available all the year round.

These grevilleas are backed by heath banksia (*Banksia ericifolia*), another plant for nectar-feeding birds. Bushy and dense, it also provides nesting sites for all sorts of birds. Next to the banksia, in the corner of the garden, is blueberry ash (*Elaeocarpus reticulatus*), a tree for fruit-eating birds. Beneath it, blackthorn (*Bursaria spinosa*) brings insect and fruit-

eaters. Its spiky leaves provide protection and it is a favourite nesting site.

Clambering along the fence line are three climbers: *Clematis aristata* forms a dense cover for small birds to nest within, while sweet morinda (*Morinda jasminoides*) and apple-berry (*Billardiera scandens*) provide fruit.

At the far end of the lawn a small waterfall runs into a shallow pool; the pump that drives it is hidden among rocks and foliage. Most of the plants in this area have strappy or grass-like leaves and are planted in groups. A drift of kangaroo paw (*Anigozanthos*) provides birds with nectar from the magnificent flowers, while cordrush (*Restio tetraphyllus*), fountain grass (*Pennisetum alopecuroides*) and zebra grass (*Miscanthus sinensis* 'Zebrinus') bring seed-eating birds.

An impressive feature here is the stand of grass trees (*Xanthorrhoea australis*) — a group of three on stout trunks in a raised bed. Their dense skirts of thin grass-like leaves are a favourite nesting site for small birds, and the spear-like flower spikes drip with nectar, attracting birds and insects alike.

Swamp banksia (*Banksia robur*) and waratah (*Telopea speciosissima*), like living sculptures, provide an interesting backdrop to this scene of fine-foliaged plants. Their impressive flowers are much loved by nectar-feeding birds, as are the flowers of the nearby prickly spider flower (*Grevillea juniperina*) and mountain devil (*Lambertia formosa*).

More water for drinking and bathing is provided in trays placed in hanging baskets suspended from the lower branches of a red-flowered yellow gum (*Eucalyptus leucoxylon rosea*). This backyard-sized eucalypt produces copious amounts of nectar over a long flowering time, as well as plenty of seeds and armies of insects. It also makes a good lookout and ideal launch pad from which to dive into the compost bin for live morsels. Beneath the yellow gum is seed-producing false sarsaparilla (*Hardenbergia*

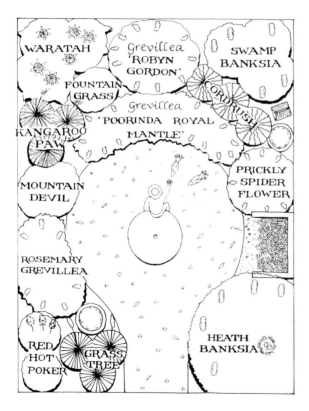

A selection of compact plants has been chosen for this smaller Bird Garden. Many of them serve two or more purposes.

violacea), and a kangaroo vine (*Cissus antarctica*) — a groundcover with black fruit that looks like grapes.

The other tree on this side of the garden is a lillypilly (*Acmena smithii*), which has fleshy fruit and nesting sites within its dense cover. Beyond its canopy is a nectar-fest: red salvia, *Grevillea* 'Robyn Gordon' and red hot poker (*Kniphofia*). These, like all other plants in the garden, are given a thick mulch of compost and leaf litter in mid spring and again in early autumn if necessary. This keeps the plants in optimum health and produces an explosion of worms and insects — a nonstop living banquet.

The Bird Garden is designed to provide a view from the house and from the adjoining patio. With the exception of sunflowers, red hot pokers and red salvia, all the plants in this plan are Australian natives which will attract a variety of birds throughout the world. But, wherever you live, be sure to search out local species, because they are the best possible plants for your neighbourhood's birdlife.

A Smaller Bird Garden

The idea of a grassy glade surrounded by trees and shrubs can be created in miniature and still bring birds. Take great care, however, in the selection of larger plants — make sure they do not dominate the area. It is better to have many small plants that satisfy a variety of needs than one large plant that satisfies few. Include a small tree if you can.

In a small version of the Bird Garden, each plant should justify the amount of space it occupies. The bigger the plant, the more enticing it should be. Look for species that are food plants and nesting sites in one. Erect as many nesting boxes as you can.

Finally, be sure to include water. Remember that a good pool or birdbath has the potential to draw every bird species in your area, regardless of its diet. Add a steady stream of water or a fountain to make it even more irresistible. Birds are not quick to forget a good bath and may pencil in your place for regular visits.

A Tiny Bird Garden

Birds will visit even the tiniest garden if they know they can feed and drink there. The first visit is the most important. Your chances are greatly increased if there is somewhere for them to perch such as a nearby tree or even a balcony railing.

Red salvia, kangaroo paw, *Grevillea* 'Robyn Gordon', swamp banksia and most grasses are suitable for pots, while blueberry ash and lillypilly can be grown in large tubs. Bird-attracting plants for window boxes and hanging baskets include fuchsias, nasturtiums, salvias, snapdragons, petunias, bergamot (*Monarda didyma*) and dwarf varieties of kangaroo paw. Red and orange varieties are usually the most successful. Place water in shallow trays and put these in the bottom of hanging baskets.

For a room with an ever-changing view, collect a few handfuls of seed from your potted collection of local grasses and other plants, and sprinkle them on trays suspended outside windows.

Chapter 7

The Butterfly Garden

This plot of orchard-ground is ours;
My trees they are, my sister's flowers;
Here rest your wings when they are weary;
Here lodge as in a sanctuary!

William Wordsworth (1770–1850), *To a Butterfly*

Perhaps the most elusive and challenging of all the visitors to the garden is the butterfly. Think of butterflies as stringless kites, miniature kinetic sculptures, tiny aerial dancers. Some dance with a lazy glide, others dart and prance, and each has its own particular flight pattern when chased. Prince Charles describes them as 'mobile flowers' and has devoted a large part of his garden, at Highgrove in the Cotswolds, to attracting them, and it is easy to see why.

A Butterfly Garden is a valuable addition to the gardenscape — both for its aesthetic appeal, and for the tiny undemanding residents that come with it, who might even introduce themselves by landing on your skin. Their gentle and endearing tickles, rather than being accidental, are actually an attempt to extract minerals from your perspiration.

Every part of the world, no matter how hot or cold, has its own unique group of butterflies. There are thousands of species, many with tantalising names: blue triangles, chequered swallowtails, fiery jewels, glasswings, zebra butterflies, question-marks, painted ladies, cloudy wings, sleepy dusky-wings.

Sadly, many of the world's butterflies are disappearing. Hundreds are endangered and some species are lost forever. International action may be necessary to save tigers, rhinos and whales, but saving the butterflies is one cause where individuals can truly make a difference: almost any sunny garden can become a butterfly sanctuary.

The ideal place to establish a thriving Butterfly Garden is a sun-drenched spot that is protected from strong winds. The warmth of the sun makes

A sheltered, sun-drenched place is the ideal setting for a Butterfly Garden filled with nectar-rich flowers. Always include buddleia — also known as butterfly plant — and watch the butterflies queue.

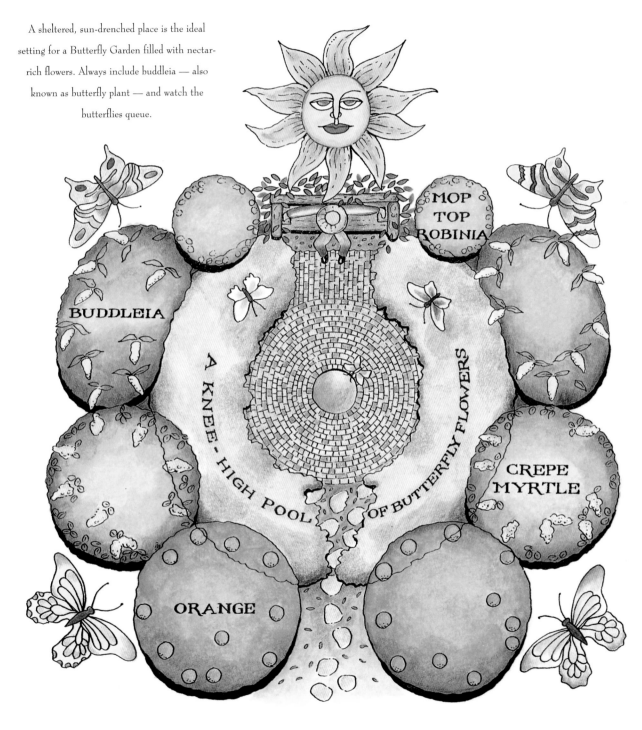

MOP TOP ROBINIA

BUDDLEIA

A KNEE-HIGH POOL OF BUTTERFLY FLOWERS

CREPE MYRTLE

ORANGE

POTTED CITRUS

A KNEE-HIGH POOL OF BUTTERFLY FLOWERS

Include phlox, thyme, achillea, scabious and wild strawberry to send butterflies into a frenzy.

butterflies active, and most of their favourite plants are sun lovers too.

Generally speaking, butterflies enjoy a bit of chaos about the place, with hiding spots and a carnival of flowering plants toppling over each other. They like a place where they can do a flower crawl without too many long-distance hauls. In fact, butterflies really appreciate the gardener who lets things go a little wild — the sort of gardener who will tolerate a few weeds here and there. White clover, a common lawn weed, is one of the butter-fly's fancies; purple top, Scotch thistle and milk-weed are other plants we consider to be weeds that butterflies find hard to resist. There are also plenty

of non-weed plants that are attractive to gardeners and butterflies alike.

A successful Butterfly Garden always has an abundance of nectar-rich flowers. Nectar is butterfly fuel for flight, and they need plenty of it, so this makes the cottage garden one of the most butterfly-friendly styles. With good plant choice there is nearly always something blooming and much to explore. And because most are relatively low-growing, cottage garden plants are also good for butterfly-watching: the butterflies are easy to see as they sip their nectar daiquiris in the sun.

The plant selection for this type of garden is enormous: heliotrope, salvia, coreopsis, lavender, phlox, cosmos, impatiens, lantana, sweet violet, *Rudbeckia hirta,* catmint (*Nepeta* x *faassenii*) and Michaelmas daisy (*Aster novi-belgii*) are just a few of the possibilities. Complement these with thistles, local grasses and wildflowers for a superb meadow guaranteed to have butterflies sailing in from every direction. Larger-growing azalea, blueberry and abelia, and vines such as scarlet runner bean, passionflower and passionfruit make good lures for passing butterflies too.

But of all the butterfly-attracting garden plants, there is one that stands out above the rest — buddleia. Known as the butterfly bush for good reason, butterflies seem to queue up for its plentiful nectar. The flower spikes, like drooping cones, weigh heavy on the branches. And just one whiff of buddleia's flower gives a clue to the honey-sweet sensation that is offered in such abundance by this wonderful plant.

Every butterfly garden with space for a medium-sized shrub needs a buddleia, or maybe even a collection of them. A large range in species, varieties and flower colour means you will be limited only by the amount of space you can devote to these easily grown shrubs. The most commonly grown species, *Buddleja davidii,* is a good choice as it flowers throughout the warmer months, when butterflies are most active.

Anyone who is interested in using their backyard as a tiny wildlife habitat will want a buddleia for the other creatures it attracts as well: all sorts of interesting insects seek out its nectar, and the red and orange varieties also attract birds. In fact, birds and butterflies share many other plants as well, including Australian natives such as acacia, banksia, grevillea, bottlebrush (*Callistemon*), grass tree (*Xanthorrhoea australis*) and lillypilly (*Acmena smithii*).

Nectar is not the only thing we need to provide for happy butterflies: if we are to have plenty of adults, we need to feed 'young butterflies' — the caterpillars — as well. Sweet violet, dill, fennel, parsley, passionflower, passionfruit, Queen Anne's lace, citrus and rue (*Ruta graveolens*) are amongst the strictly leaf-eating caterpillar's favourite fare; thistles and milkweed do double duty as larval food and nectar for adults as well. These types of plants make the garden a butterfly nursery of expectant mothers and butterflies-in-waiting. And butterfly caterpillars rarely cause much damage — a few chewed leaves here and there are a small price to pay for the pleasure of having butterflies around.

To really enjoy the butterflies in your garden, be sure to add a seat. Butterflies are not shy of 'watchers'. An accompaniment to keep on your seat could be a Butterfly Journal — a kind of butterfly 'visitors book'. Each time you see a new species you can record it, along with thumbnail sketches, plants visited and the time of year.

Such details will help you to attract more winged beauties. You will discover which flowers and plants are the most successful, and you will be able to monitor the success of each new plant addition. A good butterfly guide will help you identify every butterfly you see, rare and common. Over time, with planning and a little luck, you will have a long list of butterfly species you have successfully enticed. Each journey into the garden will be a chance to spot something new. The journal will become a valuable part of the life and history of your garden.

Plan for a Butterfly Garden

The Butterfly Garden needs a large space that basks in the sun. This plan incorporates its own wind protection — a semicircle of trees and shrubs that forms a wall of foliage without throwing shadows on the plants within.

The garden begins with a pair of citrus trees either side of a path. Their leaves are invaluable for attracting swallowtails — so called because of the extended tip on the end of their hind wing. Some swallowtails lay their eggs on citrus so you may see caterpillars on the leaves from time to time. It's worth letting the caterpillars be, as they nibble rather than ravage and rarely, if ever, do enough damage to warrant control. All citrus are butterfly-attracting so choose your favourite: lemon, orange, mandarin or lime, to name a few.

As you walk between these citrus trees, an enclosed garden is revealed. A series of stepping stones leads through a knee-high pool of butterfly flowers — phlox, thyme, achillea, scabious (*Scabiosa caucasica*) and wild strawberry (*Fragaria vesca*) in the sunnier parts are combined with impatiens and purple-flowered *Lantana montevidensis* in the shaded spots.

At the end of the path, the plants flow around a circular area paved with old bricks, and are joined with taller-growing plants such as heliotrope, lavender, artemisia, *Indigofera australis* and Michael-mas daisy. Popped in amongst them, just for fun, is

a plant that looks like hovering pink and white butterflies — gaura, the butterfly plant.

Buddleia and crepe myrtle form a background to these plantings and complete the semicircle started by the citrus trees. Buddleia provides nectar for adults, while crepe myrtle is larval food. Butterflies lay their eggs nearby so the newly hatched caterpillar's favourite food is close at hand.

A pair of mop top *Robinia pseudoacacia* 'Frisia', another larval food plant, stands either side of the Secret Butterfly Garden's butterfly bower. This plant's yellow-green leaves, in a compact ball, lend the garden an elegant, formal air.

The bower itself is a fragrant haven clothed in Chinese star jasmine (*Trachelospermum jasminoides*) with sweet violet and pinks (*Dianthus*) at its base. Chinese star jasmine attracts the oleander butterfly; its chrysalis is a shining jewel of silver or gold and is sometimes attached to the vine.

Finally, in the centre of the garden, a small unlined pond is the site for butterfly frolics. Nectar is just part of the butterfly's all-liquid diet; the other favourite is mud. Butterflies love to congregate in muddy spots — sucking the mud in and spitting it out again. Called 'mud puddling', it seems this males-only affair is about taking minerals from the soil. For whatever reason, it certainly makes for great theatre.

A Smaller Butterfly Garden

There are three ways to prune the Butterfly Garden to fit a smaller space. The first (which will leave you with the largest garden of the three alternatives) is to take off the outer circle of shrubs and trees — the citrus, crepe myrtle, buddleia and mop top robinia. This leaves the stepping stone pathway to the paved circular area surrounded by butterfly flowers, and the vine-clothed bower. A pair of potted citrus either side of the bower is a space-saving replacement for the robinias, and more in scale with a small garden.

As a second option, the circular paved area could become a circle of butterfly plants with stepping stones through the centre. Plant smaller growers such as phlox, thyme, achillea, scabious and wild strawberry in and around the stepping stones, and a selection of the taller species behind.

More compact again is the third alternative, in which the bower alone could be tucked into a corner and encircled with butterfly plants. Lay a carpet of wild thyme at your feet, then cram in fennel, golden marjoram, pineapple sage, sweet-scented marigold (*Tagetes lucida*) and bergamot (*Monarda didyma*). This food fair attracts people too — every plant is a delight to touch and sniff while waiting for butterflies.

A Tiny Butterfly Garden

Because many butterfly-attracting plants are compact, even the tiniest of gardens, such as a narrow bed against the wall of the house, should be able to accommodate a Butterfly Garden.

Many of the plants are suitable for growing in pots, so a Tiny Butterfly Garden on a balcony or verandah is also possible. Quite a few of the butterfly plants, including lavender, heliotrope and citrus, are often available as elegant standards. Blueberry is another superb pot specimen. Thyme, wild strawberry and *Lantana montevidensis* cascade impressively from hanging baskets.

If you have a sunny window, beautify your outlook on life with a window box jam-packed with some of the butterfly's favourite annuals. Throw out the rule book on colour combinations when creating your Butterfly Window and be as bold and bright as you like. Portulaca, cornflower, petunia, ageratum, alyssum, verbena and polyanthus are proven favourites. Small-growing varieties of lavender, such as *Lavandula stoechas*, are also suitable. If you have access to a garden, place a buddleia a flutter away and enjoy the fragrance as you await the show — perhaps on a window seat built especially for the purpose.

Finally, why not turn the nature strip outside your front boundary into a butterfly paradise. This improves your streetscape, and the entire neighbourhood can delight in the clouds of butterflies you bring. Low-maintenance plants are the key to this sort of garden, and the plants should be strong and dense enough to keep out weeds.

For sunny nature strips, plant thyme, golden marjoram, heliotrope, scabious, lavender, Mexican sage and catmint (*Nepeta* x *faassenii*).

The best choices for shade include golden marjoram, golden heliotrope, impatiens, *Indigofera australis* and *Lantana montevidensis*. Impatiens and *Lantana* can also be used for deep shade, as can Chinese star jasmine, either as a groundcover, or on a fence. Be sure to leave a path through the centre, at least 1 m (3 ft) wide, and consult your local council concerning rules and regulations governing the planting of nature strips in your area.

Chapter 8

The Wildlife Garden

The garden and its wildlife can be viewed
as a small part of the universe,
or, if the mind perceives deeply enough,
the embodiment of the whole universe.

Gene Logsdon (1931–), *Wildlife in your Garden*

With all the options we have for our garden, why have a Wildlife Garden? After all, we can visit a forest or nature reserve to see animals. Shouldn't the backyard be *our* haven, free of other things? This attitude has dominated Western thinking for some time — not just in the garden, but elsewhere on the planet too. Fortunately, as people begin to experience the joys of sharing their space, and to see themselves as just one of a group of many creatures, things are slowly changing.

Certainly we *could* go to a forest to enjoy wildlife at close range, but backyard adventures are so much more thrilling. We expect to be startled in a natural area, but when we come face to face with something wild in our own garden it can be a moment of unforgettable excitement, sometimes even one of terror.

It must be said that a Wildlife Garden by no means ensures an endless parade of incidents and surprises. The entertainment is not likely to be constant, or even regular. But incidents will occur, and it is just a matter of setting up the garden so that when they do, we might be there to witness them, even if it is when we are doing other things.

Open the door to your garden and take a fresh look around. You may find you already have the beginnings of a Wildlife Garden. Look under logs, and up into trees, scratch beneath soil and check under bark, look into flowers and up into the air. Most gardens, even urban gardens, are part of a wildlife network that weaves in and around the neighbourhood. Some sections of the network are busier, more alive, than others. Not surprisingly, the most vital areas are not the tended gardens, but rather the wilder pockets and corridors. While butterflies prefer a garden on the wild side, many other animals demand it. This is not to say that a neatly trimmed garden does not have creatures — it does. But, unfortunately, these tidy affairs are most likely to be seething dog-eat-dog metropolises — a few billion examples of each of the top five garden pests — rather than happy multicultural cities and satellite townships. A garden that is allowed to develop its own life force and energy is more likely to satisfy all sorts of creatures and achieve a balance where no creature dominates.

The key to success is diversity — a variety of plants and habitats is the surest way to lay out a welcome mat to a whole range of wild things. For wildlife communities, variety is more than just the spice of life — it is its lifeblood — and nowhere is variety richer than where two environments merge.

As we saw in Chapter 6, birds tend to congregate on the edge of two or more habitats — such as the boundary of a forest and clearing. In fact, they are not the only creatures with this inclination.

'Living on the edge' may not be good for human health but in the animal kingdom it ensures survival. On the margins of two environments, animals can quickly move from one to another. For example, at the edges of wetland a frog can jump from the cover of reeds onto a lily pad to snap up mosquito larvae, then, sensing the presence of a large bird, retreat into reeds.

The principle of the 'edge effect' provides us with an invaluable shortcut to enticing a whole range of animals, many of which we know little or nothing about, simply by compressing a natural habitat into a backyard-sized version. In this simplified scenario, lawn becomes grassland, a hedge becomes brush, a cluster of trees (or even a single tree) becomes forest, and our wetland frog is transported to a pond.

In fact, a pond is one habitat no Wildlife Garden should be without. It has been said that one pool of water is worth a thousand plants because every creature needs water to survive. But a pond provides the Wildlife Garden with more than just drinking opportunities. With good planning, it can be a miniature wilderness, a complete living ecosystem and, just like the oceans in the world's ecosystem, the very beginnings of a food web — this one in your own backyard.

A well-prepared pond can attract hundreds of creatures, many of them fascinating — pond-skaters, water spiders, backswimmers, water boatmen, dragonflies, giant water bugs, frogs, even turtles if you are lucky. A terrific way to get started is by pouring in a couple of buckets of water from an established pond. This brew contains the minute first foods for larger life in the form of organisms that will set in motion the seemingly endless chain of 'hunter and hunted'.

Waterlilies are one of the most useful pond plants because they help to discourage algae by shading the pond, they give shelter to fish, and provide landing and launching pads for frogs and insects. Moisture-loving grasses and reeds at the pond's surrounds act as shelter for frogs and other small creatures.

Fish can be added after the pond has established itself, usually after a few months. It is possible for the fish to arrive themselves — via an egg deposited from the claw of a water bird, perhaps — but this is rare and normally the pond must be stocked. One 15 cm (6 in) fish for every cubic metre (3 cubic feet) of water is a good rule of thumb.

Not only are fish fun to watch, they also help to control mosquitoes by eating their larvae. But also note that even a shallow pond is a danger to small children eager to watch the fish too closely, so the pond should be fenced, or covered securely

Diversity is the key to success in a Wildlife Garden.
This plan includes wetland, grassland, forest,
clearing and brush — something to entice and
excite wildlife of every kind.

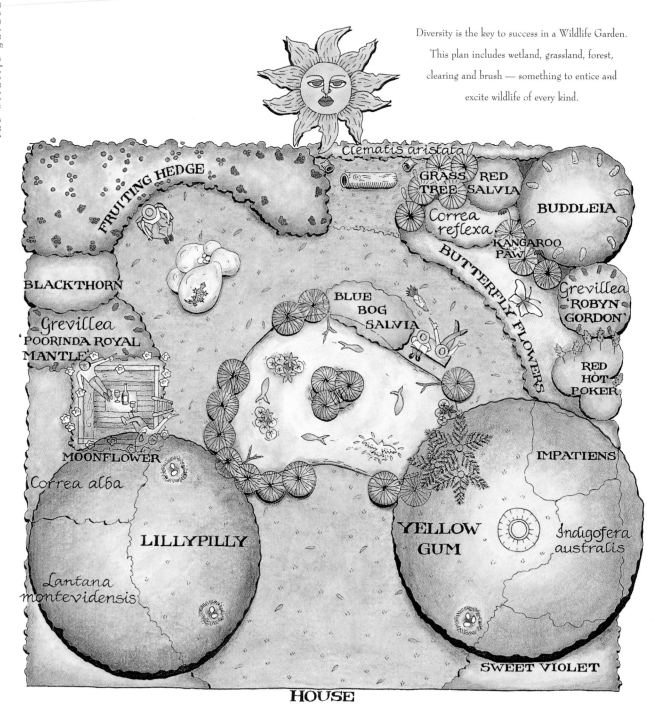

FRUITING HEDGE

Clematis aristata

GRASS
TREE

RED
SALVIA

Correa
reflexa

KANGAROO
PAW

BUDDLEIA

BLACKTHORN

Grevillea
'POORINDA ROYAL
MANTLE'

BLUE
BOG
SALVIA

BUTTERFLY FLOWERS

Grevillea
'ROBYN
GORDON'

RED
HOT
POKER

MOONFLOWER

Correa alba

LILLYPILLY

Lantana
montevidensis

YELLOW
GUM

IMPATIENS

Indigofera
australis

SWEET VIOLET

HOUSE

with strong mesh just below the water's surface. Alternatively, delay construction of the backyard pond until children are older.

A layer of mulch around pond plantings, and elsewhere too, benefits almost every creature in the garden. Its most startling impact is on the insect population which seemingly explodes overnight, providing food for frogs, birds and a multitude of other animals. Mulch also improves plant health, so animals benefit from the extra food and additional protective shelter.

Add a hollow log, if you can find one, and all sorts of wild creatures will take temporary shelter inside. Others will burrow or hibernate beneath it. Nesting boxes made from logs, as described in Chapter 6, are ideal for many other animals too. Nocturnal creatures in particular appreciate a nesting box, so make it light-proof if you can.

In your efforts to create a comfortable meeting and breeding place for a multitude of species, be sure to please that *bon viveur par excellence, Homo sapiens,* too. Have places to sit, read, meditate and relax that double as places for observation.

Scientists who study animals in the wild use screens, called 'hides', where they can watch, but cannot be seen. Sometimes these are created or erected — such as a camouflaged tent, or a pile of sticks; other times they take advantage of the existing features or natural terrain. House windows are a good hide — animals often go about their business unaware of your presence, less than a whisper away. One of the most simple open-air hides is a hammock. Lying motionless, with the hammock's sides wrapping up and around you, you can go completely unnoticed. A good book makes for a patient wildlife observer in this situation.

Another place for relaxation and wildlife-spotting is a tree house. Halfway between the earth and tree tops, you can view the action below, and get close to animals that rarely touch the ground. At dusk you can watch day creatures settle into their homes and night creatures stir, bringing a new range of sights and sounds with the darkness. And then, as at all times, your success in seeing wildlife depends on the way you use the Wildlife Garden. There is an art to wildlife-watching — it involves moving slowly, and pausing often, using your ears, and training your eyes to become aware of peripheral movement, being silent and stealthy, being witness, not master.

In all facets of the Wildlife Garden it is important to shake off the role of master. The garden and creatures within should take their own directions, without interference. You should lend only a guiding hand — to correct imbalance, dissuade the aggressive and encourage the meek.

Plan for a Wildlife Garden

In the centre of the Wildlife Garden is a pond surrounded by ferns, grasses and reeds. It has varying depths, with shallow sections around the outer perimeter for birds to bathe in. Fish nest and hide in lengths of drainpipe on the pond floor. Waterlilies, submerged in pots, float on the water's surface. An island in the middle has a small timber box surrounded by moisture-loving reeds. Lying on its side, with a thick blanket of leaves inside, the box is a home or temporary shelter from cold and storms for all sorts of creatures.

Also giving refuge to pond-dwellers and other visitors are the grassy-leafed sedges and rushes that surround the pond: *Juncus*, mat-rushes (*Lomandra*), red-fruited sword sedge (*Gahnia sieberiana*) and tassel sedge (*Carex fascicularis*). These also attract butterflies and seed and insect-eating birds and animals. Blue-flowering bog salvia (*Salvia uliginosa*) thrives here too, and is loved by insects, and all who consume them. Forked sticks pushed into the bank provide perches for birds. A bench on the banks is an ideal place for humans to relax and watch the goings-on.

Swing your legs to the other side of the bench for a view of the bird and butterfly meadow behind. Here, taller-growers including buddleia, red salvia, red hot poker (*Kniphofia*), *Grevillea* 'Robyn Gordon', grass tree (*Xanthorrhoea australis*), kangaroo paw (*Anigozanthos*) and the Australian native fuchsia *Correa reflexa* provide a background planting to smaller-growing butterfly flowers such as cosmos, honesty, heliotrope, achillea, lavender, wild strawberry (*Fragaria vesca*), pinks (*Dianthus*) and flannel flower (*Actinotus helianthi*).

In the other corner of the garden is a 'brush habitat' with a mixture of fruiting plants for birds, bats and other animals. Possibilities for this brush habitat include kangaroo vine (*Cissus antarctica*), raspberry, bramble berries (such as boysenberry and loganberry), red and white currants, or rugosa roses with their fruity hips. Blueberries are a good choice because they also attract butterflies. A seat here overlooks a group of flat stone slabs — sunbaking spots for lizards and butterflies. The seat also offers chances to see the insect and nectar-feeding creatures visit blackthorn (*Bursaria spinosa*) and *Grevillea* 'Poorinda Royal Mantle'.

Between the brush and the meadow is a 'clearing' with a hollow log on a carpet of white clover for the butterflies, bees and other insects. Apart from being a nice place to rest and relax, the hollow log is a shelter for animals, as are clay pipes three-quarters submerged below ground level. The fence behind is covered with a dense-covering climber, *Clematis aristata*, for birds to nest in.

The other side of the garden, near the house, is a woodland habitat with a tree in each corner. Two of the trees used in the Bird Garden appear here again, because of their superior food supplies: yellow gum (*Eucalyptus leucoxylon rosea*) for insects, nectar and seeds, and lillypilly (*Acmena smithii*) for fruit. Both are fitted with a range of nesting boxes. A circular seat around the eucalypt's trunk is surrounded with a carpet of shade-loving butterfly-attracting woodland plants, such as sweet violets, impatiens and *Indigofera australis*. Under the lillypilly are dense shrubs such as *Correa alba* (for birds and other nectar feeders) and *Lantana montevidensis* (for butterflies and insects).

A raised platform, amidst the outer reaches of the boughs of the lillypilly, provides a lookout over the entire garden. Reached by a ladder, and equipped with handrails and seats, this is a fragrant haven in which to while away the hours, and await action above and below. The fragrance is from nearby blackthorn and, by night, the heavenly scent of moonflower (*Ipomoea alba*) which entwines the posts and handrails and entices night-flying moths.

Although smaller, this Wildlife Garden still provides numerous habitats for a range of creatures. It includes sinuous edges, a pond, reeds, brush and meadow, and a large variety of food plants.

The Wildlife Garden incorporates a wildlife pathway extending from the hollow log, past the lookout, to the house. This pathway is created by a continuous line of dense shrubs. Animals run along its edge, looking for food, knowing they can dive for cover at the first sign of danger. The lookout is positioned at the wildlife pathway's narrowest point, providing opportunities for close observation of creatures as they pass. Rustles from a loose pile of dry leaves near the ladder of the lookout may help to indicate an animal's presence so it can be spotlit with a torch from above.

A Smaller Wildlife Garden

Each of the main wildlife habitats — the pond, reeds, brush, meadow and perhaps even the woodland — can be compressed to fit a smaller garden by choosing fewer plants for each habitat with a preference for smaller plants. For example, to establish a bird and butterfly meadow, include one taller-growing plant if you have room, but choose mainly foreground plants. When choosing plants for each habitat, aim for a balanced mix between plants with seeds, fruits, nectar-rich flowers or insect-attracting qualities.

A straight line is the shortest distance between two points, and this simple fact can be used to maximise the 'edge effect' in smaller gardens. By giving all habitats sinuous, rather than straight, boundary lines — a common practice in wildlife management — the length of habitat edges is magically expanded. This creates conditions for more abundant wildlife.

In a small garden it may be tempting to put the pond in the farthest corner, but resist this temptation. Instead, move the pond forward, so it is close to the house. Place it in a position where you can catch sight of the happenings it will host through windows as you go about household chores; or where upper-storey windows and balconies can be used as lookouts.

Frogs are in decline around the world so, with many species threatened, why not nurture a few in your garden — in their own pond. Frogs like shallow ponds less than 30 cm (12 in) deep, with reedy grasses at the water's edge, and a waterlily or two. They may arrive of their own accord, or you can collect eggs from a local pond or creek. Frog eggs are laid in masses, while toads' are laid in strings. The frog eggs soon hatch into tadpoles which, over a few months, develop into adults. Frogs also attract many beautiful water birds.

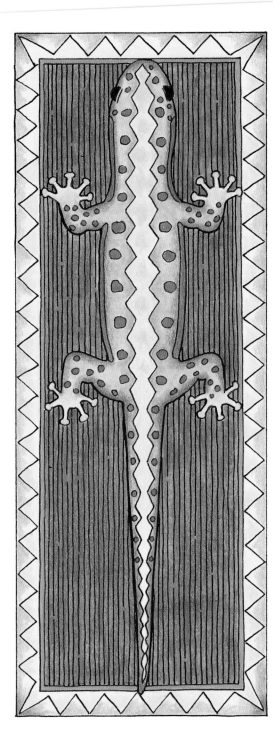

A Tiny Wildlife Garden

Even if you have the smallest of spaces in which to create a Wildlife Garden, do not go without a pond. A pond is easily achieved on a balcony or terrace, and one of the most elegant options uses a large terracotta pot. Choose a pot with a wide 'mouth' or opening. This will give the pond a large water surface for taking in oxygen — the more oxygen, the more alive your pond will be.

Place the pot in position and fill the drainage holes with sand cement. Terracotta is porous, so paint the inside of the pot with a polyurethane-based sealer. Then line the bottom with gravel or small stones, and add water plants, such as water-lilies, in pots. You will find they grow happily in pots, and are easier to maintain. To weigh them down and keep them in place, fill them to brimming with gravel.

Add water to the pond slowly and gently, including a bucketful of water from an established pond if you can. The water will be murky for the first two weeks but then it will clear. Fish can then be added. These are purchased from an aquarium shop where the staff should be able to tell you exactly how many fish are suitable for your pond's surface area.

This is a fabulous low-maintenance wildlife habitat. All it requires is a top-up with fresh water every now and then. The plants need almost no care, though the secret for a healthy waterlily is pushing a small envelope of fertiliser wrapped in newspaper into its pot every second year or so.

All sorts of creatures will come to drink at this balcony pond so make them linger with a collection of mini-habitats in large pots — perhaps to match the pond. Butterfly meadow, orchard, bird foods and bee forage can be compressed into six neat pots of zebra grass, heliotrope, lavender, blueberry, red salvia and thyme.

Passive Pleasure Gardens

GRAPE TUNNEL

FOUNTAIN GRASS

LAMB'S EAR

SILVER HELICHRYSUM

PEPPER SCENTED GERANIUM

BLUE BOG SALVIA

LEMON-SCENTED THYME

NILE GRASS

Phlomis italica

CATMINT

Artemisia 'POWIS CASTLE'

COTTAGE PINK

LEMON-SCENTED VERBENA

ARABIAN JASMINE

Rosa 'SOUVENIR DE LA MALMAISON'

GOLDEN

Rosa 'REINE DES VIOLETTES'

Rosa 'CECILE BRUNNER'

AZORES JASMINE

LAVENDER

Chapter 9

The Reading Garden

Dreams, books, are each a world; and books, we know
Are a substantial world, both pure and good;
Round these, with tendrils strong as flesh and blood
Our pastime and our happiness will grow.

William Wordsworth (1770–1850)

ife indoors can be frantic, especially in a busy household, with its inevitable interruptions and distractions, and the frenzied shrill of television, radio, music, telephones and computers. When it all becomes too much for you, it's nice to pick up a book (the excuse) and open the escape hatch (the back door).

Of all the excuses to loaf around, free from the guilt of doing nothing, reading must be one of the best. And, with the right conditions, the outdoors is the perfect venue.

Once outside, of course, you could simply collapse into the nearest seat. But a better experience awaits, deeper in the garden. Even just a few steps from the back door the pulse rate lessens. A few more steps, and half-hidden in foliage, you are beginning to relive the excitement of a truant.

By the time you turn the corner, and push through overhanging leaves into a secret garden, the house is a dim memory, and you are in another world.

Reading is often more enjoyable when you are hidden away. You can lose yourself in the pages and you are less likely to be disturbed. If you are out of sight you stand a much better chance of being out of mind as well. A few lengths of lattice and a fast-growing climber are often all that is needed to create a hideaway or, to enhance the feeling of escape and retreat, make a narrow, almost unseen entry into a voluminous space.

The space need not be enormous. A Reading Garden is most often used by only one person, sometimes two, but it is best to give an impression of space. There should be room for ideas and thoughts (perhaps tension) to disperse into the air.

After seclusion, the next consideration is comfort, and nothing is more important than having just the right mix of sun, shade and wind to fit the season. In summer we want to nestle in cool shade and feel a breeze on our cheeks; in winter we want to bask in warm sun rays away from the cool wind.

One area of the garden may change seasonally to provide a luxuriant year-round climate. If you are lucky, you may already have a sit-under tree that throws off its summer sunshade in autumn. If not, a pergola with a deciduous climber will provide similar conditions within a few years. An umbrella will do so immediately.

Another alternative is an outdoor room enclosed overhead and on three sides, facing the sun on the other — in the Southern hemisphere it faces north, in the Northern hemisphere it faces south. An outdoor room has all the comforts of indoor living without the distractions, and with the added attraction of still being part of the life of the garden. Consult an architect to design an overhang for the roof that takes advantage of the sun's seasonal pathway through the sky. In summer, when the sun is high, the room will be cast in shade; in winter, when the sun is low, it will be in full sun.

Less luxurious than a fixed reading spot, but a simpler solution, is to roam the garden, chasing the sun and shade and hiding from the winds, with a moveable chair. It can be dragged from one secluded spot to another, not just season by season, but hour by hour if you like. This also makes an ideal first stage for something more permanent — a reading garden in the making.

If this idea appeals to you, why not take an analytical approach: over the course of a year, as the seasons unfold, 'test drive' different locations around the garden. Take note of the best spots for sun and shade, where to hide from blasting winds, in fact any details that make a spot worthy for a Reading Garden. This could unearth surprises you may otherwise overlook: dewy spider webs backlit by morning sun; flickering shadow patterns from the jacaranda in summer; or a perfect winter place in the sun with oranges in picking distance.

With this research in hand, you can then choose the best single place for a Reading Garden, or use it to create a number of spots, each designed for a particular season or time of day. This allows you to have fun making the garden surrounding your Reading Garden. Flowers, tastes, scents, textures and sounds — even wildlife movements — can be woven together to create an experience to suit the season's mood. Birdsong in spring, splashing fountains in summer, rustling autumn leaves and cosy mounds of woolly thyme (*Thymus pseudolanuginosa*) in winter are just some delights you may include.

You may find that you enjoy this mobile approach to the Reading Garden. If so, create a series of level paved areas just large enough for you and your moveable seat, with shrubs or screens to make a hideaway. Alternatively, each garden could be ready-furnished with a seat or a hammock.

When choosing furniture, make comfort your highest priority. A well-proportioned table at just the right height is a must if you like to read newspapers, or to have meals, tea or coffee as you read. A seat is essential, and it needs a back rest unless you intend to put it against a wall. Aim for a seat with extra length and width, which allows you to change position now and then. The best seat is one that allows you to sit, half-recline or stretch out comfortably on your back with a pillow under your head.

To reduce the effect of sun bouncing off the page at a blinding angle, put the table in the dappled shade of a pergola or overhanging tree. In fact, glare of any sort should be avoided near the Reading Garden. Even a nearby pond might flash its twinkling eyes begging for admiration.

Finally, take time to consider what would lure you into the tranquillity of a Reading Garden — what would you hope to find in a world beyond household humdrum? You might decide, for example, to have a Reading Garden which draws on another chapter in this book as thematic inspiration. Alternatively, you could bring together a mix of favourite features from earlier chapters and those to come.

Little touches can make all the difference. Grow your own bookmarks right next to your seat: lamb's ear (*Stachys byzantina*), scented geranium (*Pelargonium*) and sweet woodruff (*Galium odoratum*) are all ideal. Sweet woodruff, which prefers to live beneath trees in cool climate gardens, has no fragrance when green, but releases a delicious vanilla fragrance when dried or pressed. No wonder it is so often found hiding between the pages of pre-loved books.

The more specifically you address your needs, whims and fancies, the more often you will find yourself, as if by accident, outside pursuing idleness and all in the guise of reading.

Plan for a Reading Garden

Chamomile swirls around stepping stones under the boughs of two fruit trees at the entry to the Reading Garden. Select your climate's most delicious species of fruit trees. For this warm temperate garden, a peach and mandarin have been chosen. Ladders rest against the tree trunks, so the fruit is easily picked on entry — as are the strawberries and blueberries in the shade beyond.

In the centre of the garden is fine grass, perfect for lying on or spreading a rug. At the far end is a pergola covered with wisteria, which has something to recommend it in every season: spring fragrance, dense summer shade, autumn leaf colour and winter sun through bare branches. Choose from Chinese wisteria (*Wisteria sinensis*) or Japanese wisteria (*W. floribunda*). The latter, with longer but often less profuse flowers, is hardier in cooler climates.

The plants that surround the grass and pergola offer a restful mix of foliage and flower colours, and other experiences too. The largest shrubs — buddleia and abelia, on either side of the pergola — are fragrant, and attract butterflies and birds. Smaller fragrant plants that bring butterflies and bees include heliotrope, lavender, thyme and bronze fennel. Cosmos and catmint (*Nepeta* x *faassenii*) bring butterflies and bees respectively, while *Grevillea* 'Robyn Gordon' brings nectar-feeding birds. Next to the pergola, the leaves of peppermint-scented geranium and lamb's ear provide fragrant and woolly bookmarks. In cool climates sweet woodruff, for its vanilla-scented bookmarks, will enjoy life under the shade of the fruit trees.

The pergola is furnished with a comfortable timber bench-seat and a table. Within easy reach a strawberry pot is brimming with herbs for tea-making: peppermint, spearmint, bergamot, golden marjoram and parsley. These, along with thyme, fennel, chamomile and mandarin peel, from elsewhere in the Reading Garden, offer an endless variety of delicious blends to sip as you read.

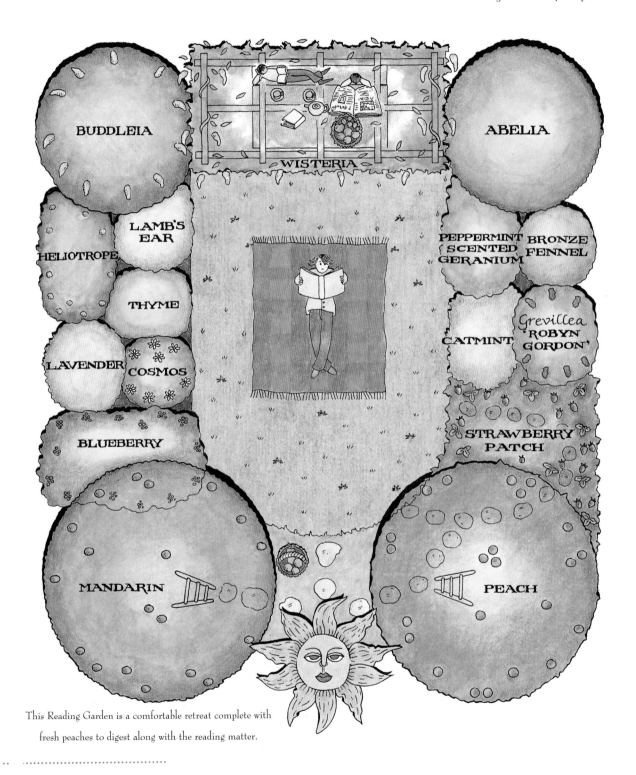

BUDDLEIA

ABELIA

LAMB'S
EAR

HELIOTROPE

PEPPERMINT
SCENTED
GERANIUM

BRONZE
FENNEL

THYME

LAVENDER

COSMOS

CATMINT

Grevillea
'ROBYN
GORDON'

WISTERIA

BLUEBERRY

STRAWBERRY
PATCH

MANDARIN

PEACH

This Reading Garden is a comfortable retreat complete with
fresh peaches to digest along with the reading matter.

A Smaller Reading Garden

The easiest way to snip this plan into a smaller shape is to leave out the large fruit trees at the entrance. Instead, have a couple of fruit trees growing in pots, or train a matching pair up either side of an arch to meet in the middle.

In tighter spaces, make the grassed area just long enough so that you can truly stretch out with a newspaper in front of you, and just wide enough so that you can roll over a couple of times without ending up in the garden beds.

Trim the pergola so that it covers the table and seat, leaving a little extra room to walk between the pergola posts and furniture. Small gardens may not have space for a buddleia, which looks its languid best when given room to spread. Abelia and mandarin, however, respond well to clipping, and can be squeezed into smaller spaces.

Sensory pleasures are even more enjoyable in these cosy surroundings so, of the smaller plants in the larger plan, give preference to plants which offer experiences: lamb's ear to pick and stroke; lavender and peppermint-scented geranium to brush past; strawberries and blueberries to taste; and vanilla-scented heliotrope to perfume the air.

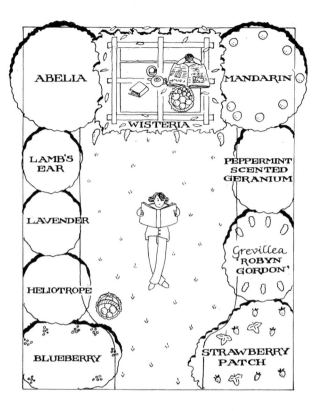

The size of the pergola and grassed area is reduced but the sense of seclusion is maintained in this plan for a smaller Reading Garden.

A Tiny Reading Garden

A tiny version of the Reading Garden may include no more than the pergola part of the plan, but even then it is worthwhile testing out and taking notes on every potential location before making a final decision.

You may decide a moveable seat is the best option for your garden, especially if it is on a terrace or balcony. If so, consider talking to a creative carpenter about the possibility of a mobile arbour. This can give you many of the benefits of a pergola, such as a sense of seclusion and protection from wind and sun, in a fraction of the space. And, if necessary, it can be tucked away somewhere, in the garage, for instance, when you need the extra space for parties and entertaining.

One possible design could be a timber construction with a bench-seat, a roof, an enclosed back wall for wind protection and handles either side. Or, for easy one-person manoeuvrability, it could have handles at one end and wheels at the other — making it as easy as a wheelbarrow to move as you follow the sun and shade, or turn your back on the wind.

Chapter 10

The Resting Garden

Here at the Fountains sliding foot
Or at some Fruit-trees mossy root,
Casting the Bodies Vest aside
My Soul into the boughs does glide:
There whets, and combs its silver Wings;
And till prepar'd for longer flight,
Waves in its Plumes the various Light.

Andrew Marvell (1621–1678)

The idea of the garden as a resting place seems to go back to the very beginnings of gardens; the Roman writer Pliny the Younger wrote of a resting place in his own garden — an alcove with a couch from under which fountains sprang.

Many contemporary gardens lack a simple place to unwind, even though such a place seems to have more relevance now than ever before. This is especially so considering modern-life pressures, and evidence from medical research that relaxation may actually bump the immunity system into high gear.

In fact, incorporating a resting area into the garden makes sense as part of a general approach to personal well-being. Here, in the fresh air and sunshine, rejuvenation is 'on call' — when we need it, as soon as we need it. No airplane ticket or hotel booking is required.

There is no single formula for a Resting Garden; the where, why and how differs from person to person, so the making begins not with the garden, but with ourselves.

First, you must ask yourself what you need. What sort of garden suits you, your nature, character and personality? Do you like to be tucked away, or within reach of the house? If you prefer the latter, are you likely to be distracted? What constitutes rest for you? Is it sitting on a bench-seat and meditating, lying on a rug watching clouds scud across the sky, or swinging in a hammock with drink in hand? Do you find it difficult to rest? If so, how can you make it easier? What temptations can you offer yourself? Once you have answered these questions, you may find a Resting Garden beginning to take shape in your imagination.

To help your imagination along, recount some of your most idyllic outdoor resting experiences. They need not be in a garden. They may be in a park, or on a holiday. Recall as many details as possible: the sun, shade, breezes, plants, scents, sounds, colours, sensations, even the size and shape of the space. Then, perhaps, draw inspiration from memories of restful interior spaces. Memories of a cathedral with soft light through stained glass and the smell of incense, say, could provide ideas.

Use these memories as springboards to dreamy possibilities: a four-poster bed with grape chandeliers and a luxuriant patchwork quilt of thyme; a rowboat brimming with chamomile sailing on a sea of frothing green; a chaise longue fashioned from calming herbs. Let your imagination run free. Later, perhaps, rein it in to fit the space and mood.

With a head full of ideas, explore the garden to find the best location. As you walk around you may be surprised at how many different microclimates your garden offers. Even the smallest garden has sun traps, cool shady spots, places blown by winds which race along narrow alleys, and pockets where warm air stands still.

The Resting Garden demands the most luxurious climate your garden offers. Find the place with the maximum number of comfortable hours each day. If you have a few options, look for details such as a view or well-placed trees for a hammock. Or you may choose various locations to be used according to the season, weather or time of day.

Once you have decided on a place, make it even better. Firstly, extend its useable seasons and hours. Thin the branches of overhanging trees if lack of light is a problem. Erect a pergola or arbour, or plant a fast-growing tree if you need shade. Block wind with a hedge, wall or fence.

Next, eliminate any distractions. Shield the area from neighbours and passers-by who may see your blissful solitude as a cry for company. If you're a compulsive gardener, make sure the most labour-intensive areas are out of sight.

The furniture is added next. Your earlier findings may help you here. Consider all options, from seats and hammocks, and more creative furniture-like ideas, as well as surfaces to stretch out on.

Then take a look at the surroundings. Is extra planting needed, or is it just right the way it is? If you have made a space within an established garden that already has a restful atmosphere, proceed with care. When faced with an overgrown jungle, it is tempting to clear, but it is often far better to tame. As Edna Walling said, 'Never can one recapture that spell of tangled mystery.'

Most gardens benefit from at least a few extra plantings, however. In such cases you can play with sensory qualities, like colour, and other plant features which will enhance the quiet mood.

When we think of restful colours, muted shades often come to mind. But even in quiet hues, not all colours of the spectrum are as restful as others. In their ongoing quest to 'twiddle our knobs', mass marketers and stress management professionals have unearthed a palette of colours which tend to calm and soothe: green, blue, blue-green, violet, pink and, sometimes, white. Each, they say, is a little different in its effect. Green calms the nerves; blue and blue-green induce a passive, dreamy state; violet brings introspection, inner balance and peace; pink is associated with tranquillity, composure and serenity; and white's effects vary from calming to somewhat cold.

Aromatherapy may have lessons for the garden-maker too. A number of scents are reputed to have a calming effect, so you may like to include them in and around the Resting Garden: jasmine, rose, lavender, tangerine, lemon balm, chamomile and sweet marjoram. Your memories of fragrances may be even more potent, so be sure to include scents that have pleasant associations for you.

Add gentle sounds, wind chimes and trickling water. If your garden has a problem with external noise, water sounds in particular may be the answer. By locating the sound as close to your ear as possible, you may replace loud, disturbing noise with something soft and melodious.

In fact, if you have room, a pool of water is well worth adding, just for the pleasure of looking at it. As Mirabel Osler said in *A Gentle Plea for Chaos*, 'Water is compulsive; it draws each of us to gaze transfixed in a becalmed state which few other things induce so forcibly.'

Plan for a Resting Garden

In this Resting Garden, the journey is part of the experience. Each step along the way aims to gently settle and soothe the senses into calm submission.

The journey begins with the lush green shade of a grape tunnel. At the end of the tunnel the sound of a fountain can be heard but its source is obscured by a drift of blue bog salvia (*Salvia uliginosa*). This is bounded either side by stands of Nile grass (*Cyperus papyrus*). The path sweeps left and right. Taking the path to the right, we find soft-textured plants in calming shades and tones: Mexican sage (*Salvia leucantha*) with its softly furry stems and violet flowers; downy lamb's ear (*Stachys byzantina*) with rosy-violet flowers; the soft and felty texture of peppermint-scented geranium; and *Phlomis italica* with pale silver-green, softly textured leaves and pink-mauve flowers. A sweep of clove-scented cottage pinks (*Dianthus*), chosen in restful shades of pink and violet, huddle at the base of *Phlomis* and neighbouring *Artemisia* 'Powis Castle'. A mass planting of dusky-pink-plumed fountain grass (*Pennisetum alopecuroides*) sways behind this scene.

And then the fragrance begins — a perfume, blended in the air, of scents reputed to calm and

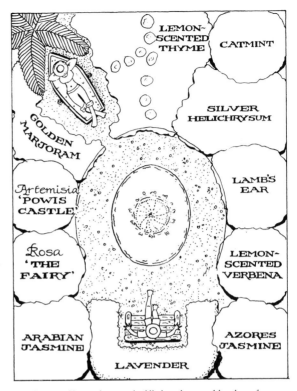

Beach yourself in a chamomile-filled rowboat and let the soft scents, hues and textures of this smaller Resting Garden soothe your senses.

soothe. Arabian jasmine (*Jasminum sambac*) throws out its arms to *Rosa* 'Reine des Violettes'. Almost thornless, its flowers, which open purple and fade to soft violet, blend beautifully with the lavender hedge that wraps around a garden seat.

The seat is positioned for contemplation of the garden and its large central pool. Directly in front is a fountain, with an island of palm trees behind. To the left, sawn-log stepping stones peep above the water to form a sweeping curve from path to island. To the right an old rowboat (with drainage holes in its hull) is half-buried in a sandy 'spit'. It is brimming with chamomile — an irresistible invitation to stretch out in the sun on a cool day.

the resting garden

The sandy spit is surrounded by golden marjoram, roses and jasmine. The chosen roses, 'Cecile Brunner' and 'Souvenir de la Malmaison', both have continuous pale pink blooms. Those of 'Cecile Brunner' are tiny and sweet-scented, while 'Souvenir de la Malmaison' has larger, stronger-perfumed flowers. Between them is Azores jasmine (*Jasminum azoricum*). Often seen as a shrubby climber, it is deliciously perfumed through summer and autumn. Here it is clipped to form a shrub.

Continuing around the path we come to lemon-scented verbena (*Aloysia triphylla*), followed by catmint (*Nepeta* x *faassenii*), lemon-scented thyme (*Thymus* x *citriodorus*) and heliotrope, for the gentle drone of bees. These have a billowing backdrop of silver helichrysum (*Helichrysum petiolare*).

The island's hammock is a place to snooze and be lulled by the murmur of grasses and the tinkling fountain under a 'forest' of palm species to suit local conditions. Wine palm (*Butia capitata*), one of the most adaptable, has edible, fragrant apricot-like fruit which can be used to make wine.

A Smaller Resting Garden

Any one of the main elements can be used singly or in combination to create a smaller Resting Garden. For example, the hammock could be used next to a wall fountain, or a small pool with a fountain. The rowboat could become the centrepiece of a garden with a selection of the fragrant and soft-textured plants chosen from the larger plan. If you prefer a more upright posture when resting, the seat surrounded with lavender could become the main feature of a smaller garden, perhaps overlooking a small pond and central fountain.

A smaller space may need smaller roses. If so, substitute more compact varieties for those in the larger plan — the beautiful pale pink polyantha rose 'The Fairy' grows to only one metre (3 ft) tall.

A Tiny Resting Garden

If you have access to a tiny square of garden, tuck the chamomile rowboat into the corner near a fence, then cover the fence with swags of a climbing jasmine, such as *Jasminum polyanthum*, or the less invasive *J. nitidum*. For sun protection in warmer months, a sail cloth may be stretched overhead. If space allows, the pool can become a tiny pond with a single spout creating a fountain in the centre.

On a balcony, a hammock is one of the most restful options. Surround it with potted plants to create a calm of colour, sound, texture and scent. For fragrance, lavender, smaller roses (such as 'The Fairy'), standard roses and jasmine can be grown in pots, as can catmint, heliotrope and thyme for the hum of bees. For soft texture, try lamb's ear, peppermint-scented geranium and Mexican sage in pots. Golden marjoram and lemon balm, for fragrance, make good hanging basket specimens and cascade out of window boxes.

The central island is a key element in this
Resting Garden plan. Get away from it all
suspended above your cares in a hammock.
Swing gently in the shade of lush palm trees
to the sound of trickling water.

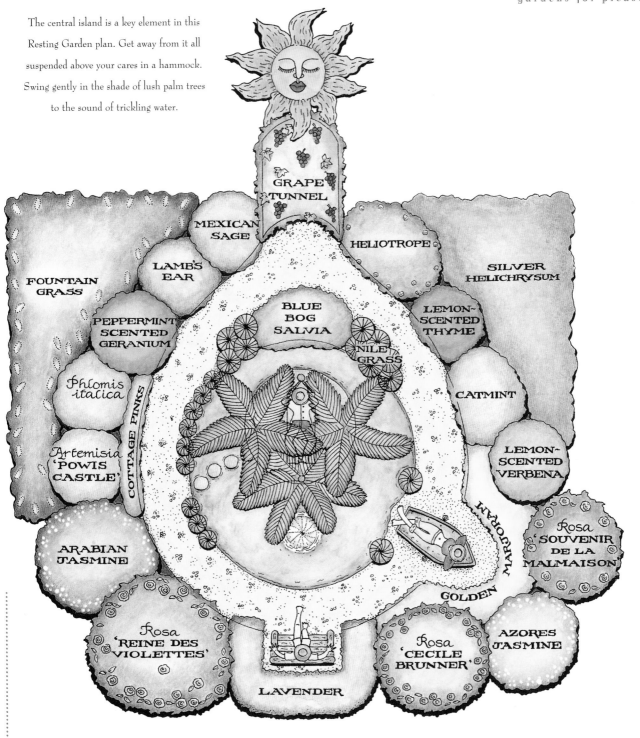

GRAPE
TUNNEL

MEXICAN
SAGE

HELIOTROPE

LAMB'S
EAR

SILVER
HELICHRYSUM

FOUNTAIN
GRASS

BLUE
BOG
SALVIA

LEMON-
SCENTED
THYME

PEPPERMINT
SCENTED
GERANIUM

NILE
GRASS

Phlomis
italica

CATMINT

Artemisia
'POWIS
CASTLE'

COTTAGE PINKS

LEMON-
SCENTED
VERBENA

Rosa
'SOUVENIR
DE LA
MALMAISON'

GOLDEN MARJORAM

ARABIAN
JASMINE

Rosa
'REINE DES
VIOLETTES'

Rosa
'CECILE
BRUNNER'

AZORES
JASMINE

LAVENDER

69

Chapter 11

The Bathing Garden

The place of greatest attraction ... was the summer bath.
It seemed to comprise everything of seclusion, elegance ...
filled with the clearest water, sparkling in the sun,
for its only canopy is the vault of heaven ...

Sir Robert Ker Porter (1777–1842)

Until the eighteenth century, even in many of the world's cooler countries, bathing outdoors was common practice. And nowhere was it more luxurious than in Persia. There, within vast court-yards, the bath was the focal point of a glorious garden. According to the painter and writer Sir Robert Ker Porter, who visited Persia early in the nineteenth century, the bath was huge, circular, and often made of pure white marble. It was surround-ed with little chambers 'furnished with every refinement of the harem' and 'a thousand flowers breathing around'.

In a world where our senses, indeed our souls, often need awakening, few experiences are as exhilarating as bathing under the skies. And there are benefits to the environment, plants and soil-life too: water goes into thirsty soil where it is needed, rather than down the drain; another reason why, it seems, the Bathing Garden should not be a thing of the past, but rather an idea for our times — a custom well worth reviving.

With a Bathing Garden, you can have all the luxuries of an indoor bathroom and more: dry space for towels and clothes, a comfortable place to stand, a mirror, even an antique basin, strewn with floating rose petals, if you like. At the same time you get the health benefits of fresh air and sunshine, along with all the sensory treats and entertainment your garden has to offer.

If you plan the set-up well enough, you may even find that the outdoor bathing area begins to replace the indoor bathroom as the favoured place for washing, especially during the warmer months of the year.

The decision between bath and shower will be made for you if you can procure a bath with style and panache. Old cast-iron claw-foot baths are somewhat scarce these days, but for the outdoor bather they are a good find indeed. If you have one, or know where one is submerged in a tangle of weeds in the back corner of a garden, by all means drag it out and scrub it down. Then use it as the centrepiece — a bay of tranquillity — in your own personal oasis.

To be used regularly, the bath needs a sunny position protected from winds and breezes. Screen the area from the outside world, preserving any good views or outlooks if you have them. Then surround it with fragrant plants. Include traditional bath herbs, such as lavender, rosemary, lovage, peppermint, thyme, chamomile, sweet marjoram and lemon-scented verbena (*Aloysia triphylla*); and roses, too, with thorns out of reach. Then, whenever you bathe, pick a selection of these herbs, mix them in a nylon stocking and run hot water over them to release the oils. Or simply reach out and pull off fresh herb sprigs to scatter on the water's surface, along with handfuls of rose petals — a bather's most luxuriant companions.

This is a place to be alone, to meditate and to find inspiration. What could be nicer than submerging yourself neck-deep in a calming potpourri? Only, perhaps, going right under for a moment and having the whole world disappear behind a veil of fragrant petals and leaves.

The other option, of course, is a shower garden. For this you need not have a lot of space — think in terms of about the size of a bathroom shower. All you need is a bit of elbow room. And a completely level area is not necessary either, as long as a level surface can be created, using decking if necessary. With a little imagination anything is possible. You could even shower on a craggy rock face, with a ladder to a timber platform. But, like

the outdoor bath, the most restful outdoor shower is part of a wonderful garden.

To establish an outdoor shower, a sunny and level area of at least 3 metres (9 ft) square is ideal. You must also consider how you intend to use it: as a rinse-off spot, for after the beach, for example? Or is it a real alternative to the bathroom? In other words, is it complete privacy you'll be needing, or just seclusion?

If people can look down onto your garden from second-storey windows or tall buildings, you may need a roof. A pergola with a semi-opaque covering allows warmth and light to penetrate, but not the gaze of prying eyes. And for complete privacy — to shower *au naturel* — add walls as well; they may be artificial screens of timber or metal, living walls formed by plants, or a combination. Artificial screens, of lattice for example, are a space-saving option and provide instant privacy. The texture of these screens can be softened with fragrant or fruiting climbers if you like.

Living walls of shrubs generally require more space, as well as time. You may even have to wait a couple of seasons for complete privacy. But the atmosphere plants generate, giving you the sensation of being nestled in foliage, adds immeasurably to the outdoor bathing experience. Patience — and showering under the cloak of darkness — may see you through for the first few 'difficult' years.

While some plants positively thrive in the immediate surrounds of a shower garden, others do not. Plants that despise humidity, or those that will not tolerate getting their 'feet' wet will not be happy. Many Mediterranean plants, for example, look forward to long dry summer spells — and woe betide the gardener who subjects them to anything else because they retaliate with all manner of diseases and problems.

Many of the plants that enjoy living near a shower are foliage plants — ones valued for their ornamental leaves, rather than flowers. And that's lucky for us, because these evoke all the tropical splendour of green-on-green. Examples include palms, bananas, ferns, *Alocasia,* and many reeds and grasses. Planting bananas, with their paddle-like leaves, is actually one of the best options for creating a jungle-like shower garden, and in warmer climates they reward deep summer watering with plump, juicy bunches. Imagine picking bananas as you shower!

Numerous flowering plants enjoy these conditions too. Australian natives such as crimson bottlebrush (*Callistemon citrinus*) with its dazzling red spikes, and *Melaleuca decussata* with its pink-mauve flowers thrive with extra water and quickly form dense, flower-laden walls, which are also attractive to birds. Each is conveniently tall-growing too, and can be trimmed to around head height.

Smaller-growing water lovers include blue bog salvia (*Salvia uliginosa*), white-flowering rain lily (*Zephyranthes candida*), pink-plumed fountain grass (*Pennisetum alopecuroides*), and colourful cannas and irises. Mauve-spired oyster plant (*Acanthus mollis*), white arum lily (*Zantedeschia aethiopica*), ever-bright impatiens, and Australian native violet (*Viola hederacea*) all love moist and shady conditions.

The platform you stand on while showering must be safe and comfortable. Pavers, unless they are specially treated, can tend to become mossy and slippery. The best options are a raised timber platform (like a mini-deck) or stone flagging, laid so water is directed into the trench that surrounds the garden.

This trench, a handspan or more in width and at least twice as deep, gives the water a place to pool when it runs off the shower area. It is particularly important in poorly drained soils, because it helps bide time, allowing the water to percolate into the soil to be used by the surrounding plants, avoiding a flood.

The trenches, like the rest of the garden surrounding the shower, must be mulched so that no bare soil is showing. This alleviates mud-splash and erosion. Pebbles or gravel are the best lining for the trenches because water penetrates these materials quickly and easily.

When it comes to the water source for the shower, there are a number of choices. The simplest is a camper's portable shower: fill the bag with water, warm if you like, sling it in a tree or attach it to a post, and control the flow with a shower rose below. A solar-heated model provides a free hot shower when left in the sun.

Showers that attach to a garden hose can be set up in a permanent position and attached when needed. There is a wide range available, from simple, inexpensive hose fittings, to sophisticated free-standing models with built-in solar-collectors.

The most permanent option, which is perhaps also the most convenient, is a shower

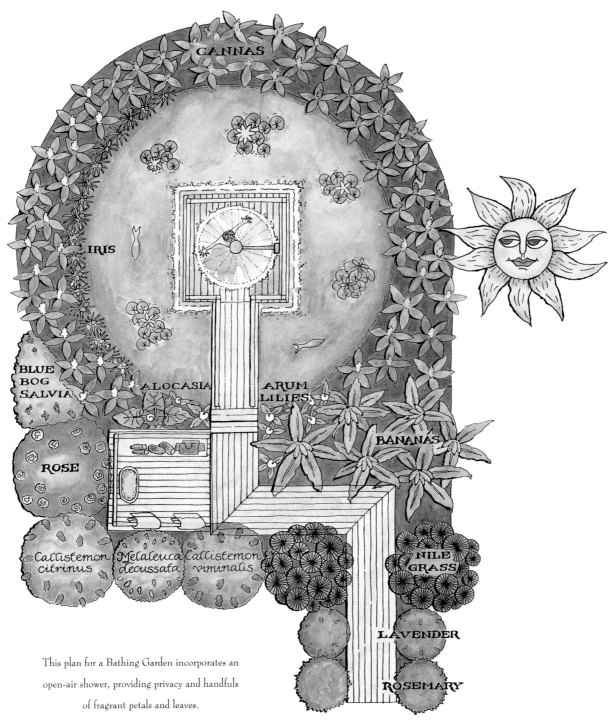

CANNAS

IRIS

BLUE
BOG
SALVIA

ALOCASIA

ARUM
LILIES

BANANAS

ROSE

Callistemon
citrinus

Melaleuca
decussata

Callistemon
viminalis

NILE
GRASS

LAVENDER

ROSEMARY

This plan for a Bathing Garden incorporates an
open-air shower, providing privacy and handfuls
of fragrant petals and leaves.

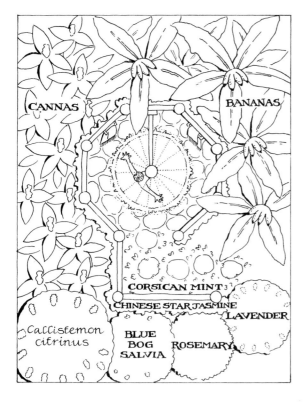

Lattice screens covered with summer-fragrant Chinese star
jasmine create a private, scented showering haven for this
smaller Bathing Garden.

they can be scented with oils, or with citronella to keep mosquitoes at bay. For the convenience of artificial lighting, the most atmospheric options include strings of fairy lights, and recessed lights set into retaining walls and paths.

Whatever design or style of Bathing Garden you choose, create a garden which, as well as being useful, is beautiful and full of sensory delight.

A Plan for a Bathing Garden

A raised timber walkway leads into the Bathing Garden or, more specifically, the Shower Garden. Mounds of lavender and rosemary mark the entry, and small flowers and sprigs of foliage can be collected on passing.

From here the garden's interior is completely hidden behind large clumps of Nile grass (*Cyperus papyrus*), and a screen of flowering shrubs including *Melaleuca decussata*, weeping bottlebrush (*Callistemon viminalis*) and crimson bottlebrush (*Callistemon citrinus*). Straight ahead is a stand of bananas. As we approach we see they are underplanted with 'Green Goddess' arum lilies (*Zantedeschia aethiopica*).

Here the walkway turns to the left, and leads to a dressing room of sorts, complete with a porcelain basin on a stand, and a mirror above it. There are handrails for towels, a long bench-seat for clothes, and a wall of fragrant summer-flowering *Rosa* 'Reine des Violettes' — its violet petals within easy reach for scattering in the washbasin. The sky-blue flowers of blue bog salvia are nearby too, along with *Alocasia* and its fruitily fragrant spathes.

From the dressing room you have a view of the shower, basking in sunlight in the middle of a small pond. The pond itself is surrounded by a dense, impenetrable planting of cannas. Arranged in clumps of white, red, lemon, apricot and pink, they

and standpipe installed by a plumber. The cost of this varies according to the shower's distance from existing pipework and the amount of labour involved, but it offers the luxury of instant water — hot as well as cold, if you like. If you are intending to use hot water in your outdoor shower, take care to turn up the cold water level when showering outside so as not to damage plant roots.

If you would like to bathe by night, add light — especially along the pathways that lead to your bathing area. Subtle lighting, to complement the moonlight, is best. Candles, lanterns and bamboo flares give a flickering light for a magical mood, and flower nonstop throughout summer. To heighten the effect, along the sunniest side of the pond is a rainbow of water-loving irises (such as *Iris laevigata*, *I. virginica* and 'Louisiana' hybrids) all dipping their toes in the water.

The shower itself is reached via a timber bridge that doubles as a fish-viewing platform, and showering produces wonderful sounds as the water falls in steady streams from the platform into the pond below.

This garden makes a unique rinse-off area adjoining a pool, or works equally well as a summer alternative to the bathroom, adjoining the house or outdoor living area.

A Smaller Bathing Garden

Create a secluded shower area using lattice screens covered in Chinese star jasmine. For complete privacy, arrange them so the entry has a twist, as in the large plan. Sprinkle scent and colour generously at the entrance with plants such as lavender, rosemary, blue bog salvia, and the lemon-scented leaves of crimson bottlebrush; and plant Corsican mint between stepping stones for a fragrant entrance path. In the shower room it-self, lay stone flagging so that the water runs into the surrounding garden beds of water-loving plants. Choose plants to fit the available space, as well as your garden's climate, from the water-loving plants already mentioned.

To preserve precious sun, take care in laying out this garden, especially when positioning large shrubs and tall, overhanging plants, such as bananas. These need to be placed where they will throw shadows away from where you will shower (that is, to the north in the Southern hemisphere, and to the south in the Northern hemisphere).

A Tiny Bathing Garden

In the tiniest garden space, create a shower room with a door, using screens of lattice or woven bamboo. Cover with a climber if you like, but be sure to choose one that benefits from the water — many (such as climbing roses) are prone to diseases in these humid conditions. Chinese star jasmine (*Trachelospermum jasminoides*) with its mid-summer fragrant flowers makes a good choice.

On a terrace or balcony, an open-air bath is often the easiest option. Before beginning, however, check with a builder that the balcony is strong enough to support the enormous weight of a bath full of water.

There are a number of ways to create privacy. One of the easiest is to use portable potted plants: choose quite densely leafed species that will grow high enough for you to hide behind, such as conifers, bamboo, lemon-scented ver-bena, lillypilly (*Acmena smithii*) and orange-scented jessamine (*Murraya paniculata*). When you have finished bathing in privacy, the potted plants can be arranged around the

perimeter of the space, against walls and balconies. This idea is made easier if the pots are placed on a plank of wood with casters beneath.

In the smallest space, you can make a portable but very private hideaway with free-standing hinged screens, or bamboo blinds which hook onto the eaves. Once you are in hiding, surround yourself with small pots of your favourite 'bath plants'. Choose from lavender, rosemary, peppermint, thyme, chamomile, sweet marjoram and, if space allows, grow any of the rugosa and patio roses suggested previously.

Interactive Pleasure Gardens

Chapter 12

The Tea Garden

Teasim is a cult founded on the adoration
of the beautiful among the sordid facts
of everyday existence.

Okakura Kakuzo (1862–1913), *The Book of Tea*

Throughout the centuries, in both the East and West, tea and gardens often appear together. And when they do, it seems, it is always to the great benefit of their users and partakers. In fifteenth-century Japan, formal tea gardens were the setting for a ritualised tea ceremony. They offered a chance to meet with friends and discuss a work of art. Later, in the great pleasure gardens of London such as Vauxhall and Ranelagh, tea gardens were part of the alfresco entertainments of the aristocracy and upper classes. And, in Victorian times, tea was taken on the lawn as part of an afternoon of games and pleasures.

Today, tea and gardens can meet again. But this time, why not put a contemporary twist in the 'tale'? Create a garden that is more than just a venue for the *taking* of tea. Bring together plants for

the *making* of tea as well. Then, whenever you or your guests feel inclined, the garden can become a place of concoctions, creativity — even tea tastings.

At first glance a Tea Garden may seem no different to any other that surrounds an outdoor entertaining area: a colourful array of plants of varying form and foliage, with plenty of flowers. But it gives much more. There's the fragrance on brushing past, then the heady scent of picking, followed by the aroma of steeping herbs and, finally, the taste, freshly brewed.

Some of the most popular herbal tea plants — and deservedly so — are lemon flavoured. They come in a variety of shapes and sizes from small shrub-sized lemon-scented verbena (*Aloysia triphylla*) and swaying lemon grass (*Cymbopogon citratus*) to mounds of lemon balm (*Melissa officinalis*) and ground-hugging lemon-scented thyme (*Thymus* x *citriodorus*). Each tastes a little different, so it is worth including all of them in your Tea Garden if you have plenty of space.

Also in a citrus vein, with one of the finest flavours of all herb teas — a blend of lemon, mint and aniseed — is bergamot (*Monarda didyma*). This is often referred to as Oswego tea — after the Oswego Native Americans who introduced it to early American colonists.

The mint flavours are another tantalising group. Spearmint, applemint and peppermint make the tastiest teas — peppermint, a relaxant, is highly recommended. Mint has a reputation for growing out of control which, unfortunately, is well justified, so it is best contained in pots, which can be sunk into the garden if you like.

Some plants make worthy inclusions because, even when used quite sparingly, they add a unique flavour to the blend. Lime-scented, nutmeg-scented and rose-scented geraniums (*Pelargonium* spp.) give tea extra body and a distinctive aroma, as does rosemary. For delicious aniseed notes, try fennel, anise hyssop (*Agastache foeniculum*) and sweet-scented marigold (*Tagetes lucida*).

Lemon, lime and orange trees are useful inclusions for their juices and also for their rind — a secret ingredient in many of the zippiest blends. Where space is limited, grow them in pots.

Chamomile tea, one of the most relaxing herbal teas, is made from the flowers of the up-right-growing German chamomile (*Matricaria recutita*) or mat-forming lawn chamomile (*Chamaemelum nobile* syn. *Anthemis nobilis*). With both it is just a matter of picking the flowers and steeping them in water. There is no need to dry them, however drying does ensure a supply even when they are not in bloom.

Rosehips — the wonderful red fruits that follow the flowers on roses — also make a soothing tea which is rich in vitamins C, A, E and B. Any rose can be used if it produces fruit, but the rugosa rose 'Fru Dagmar Hastrup', with its excellent tomato-red hips, is a good compact choice for the Tea Garden. To make rosehip tea, wash the hips, cut them in half, remove the seeds, then finely chop the fruit. Place in a saucepan of water, and boil slowly for five minutes. For extra aroma add cloves, raisins and a little lemon and sugar.

Rose petals make a delicate-tasting tea, too. Dark red roses (such as the wonderfully fragrant hybrid tea rose 'Mr Lincoln') are particularly pleasing. As the loose petals sit in the boiling water for the ten minutes the tea takes to brew, they release a cloud of colour with a mouthwatering ruby hue. Rose-petal tea can be served hot or iced, with honey to enhance the flavour. Iced tea can be brewed in jars by the sun, or made in the same way as herbal tea, then refrigerated after brewing.

While we are in the realm of iced tea, consider growing a few plants that bring the flavour alive. Parsley, basil and coriander, for example, provide the grassy notes that are so important. And nothing beats a fruit-infused brew on a summer's day. Try home-grown mangoes, peaches or raspberries — so good with a splash of champagne. A nice finishing touch for a frosty jug of iced tea is edible flowers, such as pinks (*Dianthus*), sweet violets, nasturtium, borage and daylily, held captive in ice cubes perhaps.

Experiment with true teas as well. There are thousands of them, yet they all come from a single species — *Camellia sinensis*. Grown mostly in Asia and Africa, it is a relative of the much-loved flowering camellias. The different flavours are a result of where it was grown, when it was picked, and how it was processed.

There are three main types: black tea, green tea and Oolong tea. Black tea, the best known in Western countries, is fermented (that's tea-talk for the oxidation process), giving it that distinctive full-bodied flavour. Tea bags, even the 'good quality' ones, are invariably filled with tea dust or fannings — the leaf particles that are sifted from full-leaf teas.

If you have rarely ventured into the waters beyond the tea bag, now is the time to visit a specialty tea shop and dive into the ocean of flavours that awaits you in long-leaf varieties. Be sure to try those which are most prized for flavour, such as delicate Assams, winy Keemans, smoky Lapsang Souchong, and Darjeeling — often referred to as the champagne of teas.

Green tea, popular in China and Japan, is unfermented. It is lower in caffeine than black tea and prized for its aroma and finesse, so it is mostly served without sweeteners, milk or lemon. A delicious exception is Moroccan mint tea — gently sweetened green tea poured over a bed of fresh, lightly crushed mint leaves. Oolong teas, from Taiwan, lie between black and green teas. They are partially fermented and often called Formosa tea.

Tea tasting can be just as exciting as wine tasting, and relatively inexpensive when you consider the cost per cup. In fact, experimenting with flavours and blends is one of the great, perhaps unexpected, delights of the Tea Garden. Think like a wine-maker. Balance and counterpoise elements of spiciness, bitterness, sweetness and sourness. Experiment with aroma and colour. Create blends for different times of the day. Record your favourite tea blends — maybe even bag them and give them your own label.

At tea tastings, have condiments on hand such as milk, honey, sugar, lemon juice, citrus rind shavings and cinnamon-stick stirrers. Make flavoured sugars by rubbing sugar cubes against citrus fruits, or placing them in a sealed container with a few leaves of peppermint-scented geranium for a day or two prior. For spice and fruit-infused iced teas include fresh ginger, cardamom pods and fruit juices, along with fruit slices, champagne and flavoursome and decorative ice cubes.

Take time to consider the best location for the Tea Garden. A position close to the house is most convenient, especially if you are relying on the kitchen for boiling water. You may find you already have the perfect setting — a functioning entertaining area that needs inspiration. On the other hand, you could take a cue from the Japanese — they tucked their tea houses into the corner of the garden, at the end of a path that led the visitor through the garden on a miniature journey, giving them things to admire and enjoy on the way.

You too may like to have a structure, such as a pavilion, for shelter from the elements — even a few creature comforts such as power points or a camping cooker, and cupboards to hold everything you need. Then you can pluck leaves and flowers and make teas, right there, in the garden.

All herbs have medicinal properties, so a few simple guidelines must be followed. Use only herbs and plants traditionally used for tea-making — some others are unsuitable, a few even dangerous. Be sure of the plant species by purchasing labelled

Grow, pick, brew and taste your favourite teas with or without ceremony in your own Tea Garden. Locate it in the centre of your backyard, or tuck it away in a private corner.

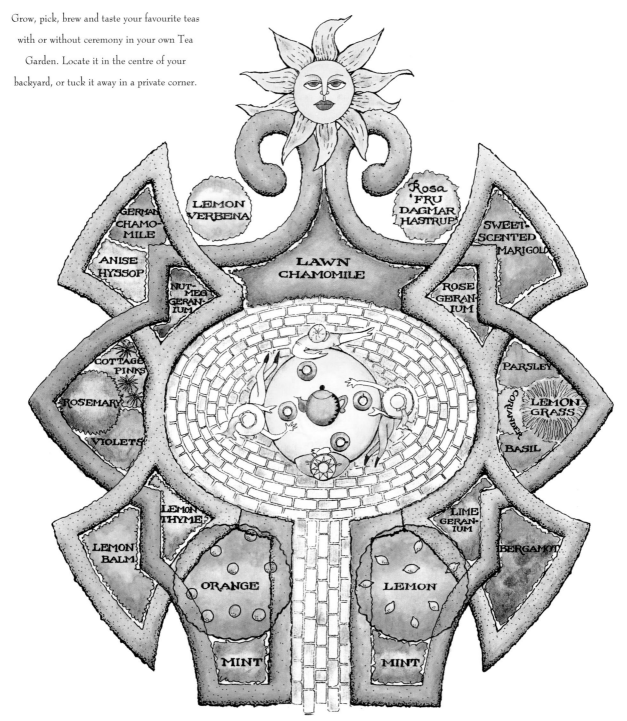

GERMAN CHAMOMILE

LEMON VERBENA

Rosa 'FRU DAGMAR HASTRUP'

SWEET-SCENTED MARIGOLD

ANISE HYSSOP

NUT-MEG GERAN-IUM

LAWN CHAMOMILE

ROSE GERAN-IUM

COTTAGE PINKS

ROSEMARY

PARSLEY

CORIANDER

LEMON GRASS

VIOLETS

BASIL

LEMON THYME

LIME GERAN-IUM

LEMON BALM

ORANGE

LEMON

BERGAMOT

MINT

MINT

plants from reputable sources. Drink a variety of herbal teas in moderation, rather than a few to excess — yet another incentive to try new brews.

The plants described here and in the following garden plans provide a safe guide to the tastiest tea plants and provide plenty of scope to experiment. In fact, you'll find there's enough flavour and variety to entertain the palate for many years, perhaps even a couple of lifetimes.

Plan for a Tea Garden

The Tea Garden is arranged as a knot garden with an entertaining area in the centre. This formal symmetrical approach, developed in Elizabethan times, is often used for growing herbs. Its effect is particularly obvious when seen from above — from buildings or a higher level of the garden.

Thyme, santolina, box (*Buxus*) and small-leafed honeysuckle (*Lonicera nitida*) are some of the best choices for the outlining hedges. (Only thyme can be used for making tea, so be sure to label plants that can't.) An illusion of overlapping threads can be created with contrasting foliage. Silver santolina or a golden or variegated thyme edging the entry path would shine at dusk and into the dark.

An orange and lemon tree, both in pots, stand either side of the path, in the entry beds. Growing around these pots, peppermint, applemint and spearmint form a carpet. To limit their spread, they are contained in submerged pots.

The brick path leads to a welcoming oval-shaped area with a table and chairs. In warmer months, a market umbrella provides shade. A huge variety of herbal tea plants is within easy reach.

To the right, with wonderful red summer flowers, is bergamot, with lower-growing lime-scented geranium (*Pelargonium* 'Nervosum') in the bed in front. Lemon grass, in the next bed, is

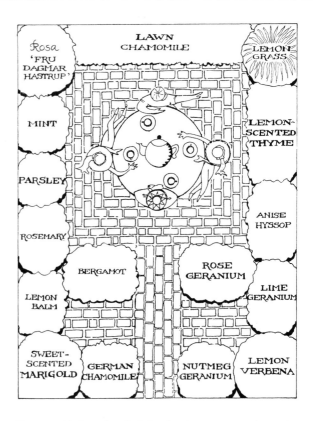

Plants suitable for making herbal and iced teas are grouped around a brick-paved entertaining area in this small Tea Garden. As well as their flavour, each can be enjoyed for their fragrance.

surrounded with herbs for iced tea — parsley, coriander and basil. The next is filled by sweet-scented marigold, so prized for its aniseed-flavoured leaves; rose-scented geranium provides a textural foreground for this scene.

To the left of the entertaining area, lemon balm is planted behind a mound of lemon-scented thyme. For added visual interest in this part of the garden, search out one of the golden cultivars of lemon balm (*Melissa officinalis* 'Aurea' or 'All Gold') and either the gold or silver-variegated lemon-scented thyme. The central bed on this side has rosemary with an underplanting of sweet violets and pinks for their edible flowers, followed, in the corner, by German chamomile, anise hyssop and nutmeg-scented geranium.

Behind the entertaining area, between the left and right-hand beds, a swathe of lawn chamomile spills onto the brick paving. It can be sat on or trodden on, and, when in flower, picked to make fresh chamomile tea. Within reach of this fragrant carpet is lemon-scented verbena, and *Rosa* 'Fru Dagmar Hastrup' for her petals and rosehips.

A Smaller Tea Garden

A smaller Tea Garden could retain the entertaining area, and reduce the garden to a less elaborate series of rectangular beds. Placed shoulder-to-shoulder, you may find there is space for almost all the plants in the large plan. Use the knot garden as your planting guide. The plants used around the outer reaches of the knot garden are taller, so place them behind others.

Alternatively, if you like the idea of a knot garden of tea plants, create a miniature version. Replace the entertaining area with a citrus in a pot, substitute ribbons of gravel or lines of bricks for hedges — these can be the tiny paths between plants. Then colour-in with plants, giving emphasis to the tastiest and smallest-growing ones, and making sure there is a swathe of chamomile — the smaller Tea Garden's 'entertainment area'.

A Tiny Tea Garden

Many tea plants are also very compact, making a Tea Garden an economical choice for tight spaces. If you have any garden at all, consider making a Tea Path. Use old bricks and leave spaces for plants here and there to spill over the edge. For a path in the sun, plant chamomile, thyme, sweet violets, parsley, basil, coriander, pinks and scented geraniums. Mint and sweet violet are suitable for shaded paths as well.

On a balcony or terrace, create a hanging Tea Garden using the smaller tea plants from the plan. Or start a collection of tea plants in pots — Tea Pots. Every plant in the plan should do well in a pot, given a sunny location, though mint prefers shade. The other alternative is one large tea pot. Small tea plants, such as mint, chamomile, thyme, parsley, basil, coriander, sweet violets and scented geraniums look divine in large strawberry pots. These terracotta planters have a planting hole at the top and several others in the sides as well, so one strawberry pot can provide the ingredients for dozens of different-tasting brews.

Chapter 13

The Posy Garden

And I will make thee beds of roses
And a thousand fragrant posies

Christopher Marlowe (1564–1593)

A Posy Garden is a great place to get amongst your plants, to wander with a pair of scissors, snipping blooms and arranging them into a bunch as fresh and informal as flowers swept up from a meadow.

In the eternal quest to find a garden that 'pays its way', few people have found one to earn its keep as beautifully as the Posy Garden. A single plant — costing less than the smallest bunch of florist-bought flowers — can provide nonstop picking for your home and your friends year after year, and one packet of seeds is capable of producing twenty times its value in cut flowers.

But the value of the Posy Garden goes beyond the economic — it also increases your options. Growing your own means fresher flowers and a greater selection than you can buy. For instance, you can grow flowers in the precise colours you desire, including those varieties florists never sell — ones so dainty they must be placed in water immediately on picking.

Every garden needs flowers for picking, even if they are tucked into a corner among other things. Whether for a last-minute finishing touch to the dinner table, a bedside posy when a guest comes to stay, or tiny 'teacup bouquets' for every room in the house, flowers from your own garden add a friendly, personal touch.

A Posy Garden can be as tiny as a group of pots or as large as your entire garden but, to be successful, it needs careful planning, particularly in the choice of plants. Not all flowers are good for picking. For some, the passage from voluptuous to vanquished is very fast indeed — many wilt and fall

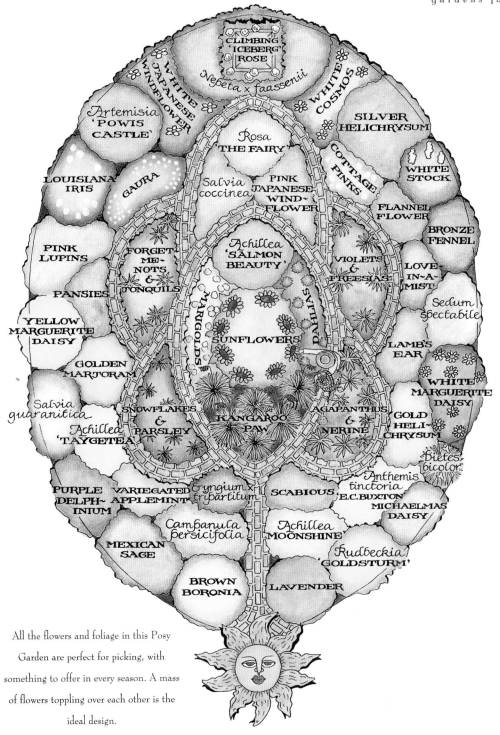

CLIMBING 'ICEBERG' ROSE

Nepeta x faassenii

WHITE JAPANESE WINDFLOWER

WHITE COSMOS

Artemisia 'POWIS CASTLE'

SILVER HELICHRYSUM

Rosa THE FAIRY

COTTAGE PINKS

WHITE STOCK

LOUISIANA IRIS

GAURA

Salvia coccinea

PINK JAPANESE WIND~ FLOWER

FLANNEL FLOWER

BRONZE FENNEL

PINK LUPINS

FORGET~ ME~ NOTS & JONQUILS

Achillea 'SALMON BEAUTY'

VIOLETS & FREESIAS

LOVE~ IN~A~ MIST

PANSIES

MARIGOLDS

DAHLIAS

Sedum spectabile

YELLOW MARGUERITE DAISY

SUNFLOWERS

LAMB'S EAR

GOLDEN MARJORAM

WHITE MARGUERITE DAISY

Salvia guaranitica

SNOWFLAKES & PARSLEY

KANGAROO PAW

AGAPANTHUS & NERINE

GOLD HELI~ CHRYSUM

Achillea 'TAYGETEA'

Dietes bicolor

PURPLE DELPH~ INIUM

VARIEGATED APPLEMINT

Eryngium x tripartitum

SCABIOUS

Anthemis tinctoria E.C.BUXTON

MICHAELMAS DAISY

Campanula persicifolia

Achillea MOONSHINE

MEXICAN SAGE

Rudbeckia 'GOLDSTURM'

BROWN BORONIA

LAVENDER

All the flowers and foliage in this Posy Garden are perfect for picking, with something to offer in every season. A mass of flowers toppling over each other is the ideal design.

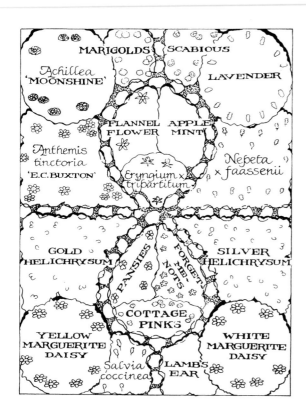

MARIGOLDS SCABIOUS

Achillea 'MOONSHINE'

LAVENDER

FLANNEL APPLE
FLOWER MINT

Anthemis
tinctoria
'E.C.BUXTON'

Eryngium x
tripartitum

Nepeta
x faassenii

GOLD
HELICHRYSUM

PANSIES
FORGET-ME-NOTS

SILVER
HELICHRYSUM

COTTAGE
PINKS

YELLOW
MARGUERITE
DAISY

Salvia
coccinea

LAMB'S
EAR

WHITE
MARGUERITE
DAISY

Stepping stones weave through this smaller year-round Posy Garden.
Golden foliage and flowers are grouped on one side of the figure-eight
path, with blue, silver and white on the other.

apart almost the moment they are picked, never making it anywhere near a vase.

The perfect posy plant is not content to let its beauty languish in the garden. It kindly lets us snip its stems and take it inside as well. It flowers for months on end with plenty for the garden as well as the vase, and rarely looks shorn, even when newly plundered. It needs little care and attention, and has a compact habit, so there is room for others as well.

This 'perfect posy plant' may sound too good to be true, but actually it's not. A surprising number of plants have such qualities, and they come in a wide range of colours. Mauve and violet hues offer a wide selection of flowers. Among the best are lavender, *Brachyscome multifida,* catmint (*Nepeta* x *faassenii*), Mexican sage (*Salvia leucantha*), stoke's aster (*Stokesia laevis*), and frilly-petalled scabious (*Scabiosa caucasica*) which sometimes borders on blue. For true blue, plant sky-blue bog salvia (*Salvia uliginosa*) and royal blue *Salvia guaranitica*.

For months of yellow flowers, include daisy-flowered *Anthemis tinctoria* 'E.C. Buxton', and *Achillea* 'Moonshine' and 'Taygetea', while *Achillea* 'Salmon Beauty' adds a mouthwatering peachy-orange. For red blooms, *Salvia vanhouttei*'s deep scarlet flowers, lined up at the ends of long swaying stems, are a match to ignite any posy. In temperate gardens, marguerite daisy in white and pastel hues is rarely without a flower. These flowers are just some of the mainstays of the Posy Garden. Consult your local nursery for others.

Be sure to include foliage plants too. Useful all year long, they bring a bunch of flowers to life. Ferns, herbs, ivy and lamb's ear (*Stachys byzantina*) are favourites, but there are three that no Posy Garden should be without: *Artemisia* 'Powis Castle', silver helichrysum (*Helichrysum petiolare*) and gold helichrysum (*Helichrysum petiolare* 'Limelight'). Each of these adds something special to a posy, and their soft textures and colours blend with almost every flower in the garden.

Endless simple arrangements are possible with 'mainstays' and foliage alone. But seasonal specials increase the repertoire and sprinkle surprises throughout the year. Winter, in particular, is worth planning for — it need not be a time of lean pickings. There are creamy-green and pink hellebores (*Helleborus*); the dainty nodding bells of snowflakes (*Leucojum vernum*) and snowdrops (*Galanthus nivalis*); flower-filled shrubs such as Geraldton wax (*Chamaelaucium uncinatum*), yellow marguerite daisies

(*Euryops pectinatus*) and primrose-yellow winter jasmine (*Jasminum nudiflorum*); and, in warmer zones, velvet-petalled violas and pansies begin blooming in winter. Add fragrance to winter posies with jonquilla hybrids (*Narcissus jonquilla*), winter sweet (*Chimonanthus praecox*) and daphne (*Daphne odora*). A few strands of these fill an entire room with fragrance.

Of spring's cutting flowers, the highest accolades go to bulbs such as tulips, fragrant freesias, daffodils, grape hyacinths and iris; scented shrubs such as roses, lilacs, brown boronia and sage-leafed buddleia (*Buddleja salviifolia*); and, of course, annuals such as delphinium, stock, poppy, sweet pea, lupins, love-in-a-mist and forget-me-not.

Many of these continue well into summer, and are joined in the vase by summer-flowering annuals such as cosmos and zinnia; perennials such as gaura, shasta daisy, *Dietes bicolor*, *Campanula persicifolia*, seaholly (*Eryngium*), pinks (*Dianthus*), flannel flower (*Actinotus helianthi*), and tuberose (*Polianthes tuberosa*); and shrubs such as *Buddleja davidii*, mock orange (*Philadelphus coronarius*) and even more roses.

In fact, some roses will continue into autumn — among them rugosa roses, hybrid musks, and others including 'Iceberg', 'The Fairy', and the climbing roses 'New Dawn' and 'Zephirine Drouhin'. Incidentally, old-fashioned roses such as these tend to have a fleeting life in the vase, so pick them in bud, or simply enjoy them while they last. Modern hybrids are longer-lasting in vases but often appear quite stiff and formal in the garden.

Other highlights of autumn include Michaelmas daisy (*Aster novi-belgii*), Japanese windflower (*Anemone* x *hybrida*), *Sedum spectabile* 'Autumn Joy', the pink-flowering bulb *Nerine bowdenii* and the golden daisies of coneflowers (*Rudbeckia*). A profusion of berries and fruit complete the circle and take the Posy Garden into winter once more, ensuring that there is never a dull moment — or an empty vase.

Consider these plants as a starting point. You are sure to want others as well — flowers, foliage, and perhaps even fruit — to suit your personal decorating tastes and schemes. For example, you can have fun colour-matching flowers with vases, curtains, paintings and furniture; or making bold floral statements with sunflowers, arum lilies (*Zantedeschia aethiopica*), agapanthus and bird-of-paradise (*Strelitzia reginae*).

If you want to explore the realm of dried flowers, along with previously mentioned achillea, seaholly, lavender, love-in-a-mist and flannel flower, add annuals such as statice (*Limonium sinuatum*), honesty (*Lunaria annua*) and everlasting daisy (*Bracteantha bracteata* syn. *Helichrysum bracteatum*).

By now it is likely that the many plants of the Posy Garden in your mind's eye have jumped the boundaries of their allotted area, and are now pushing at the fence posts. So the final question now begs: how do we arrange all these plants?

Neat rectangles against walls, and along paths, fences and driveways are one option, and a particularly good one where space is tight. But, somehow, a Posy Garden cries out for something more exciting, more chaotic — something like the type of garden Vita Sackville-West hinted at when she said: 'If I were suddenly re-quired to leave my own garden and move into a bunga-low, I should have no hesitation at all about ruffling the garden into a wild asymmetrical mess.'

A mass of flowers all in a topple is a romantic notion, and, as a design idea for a Posy Garden, it is also practical. Many of the best plants for cut flowers have lax stems but by crowding plants together, the need for staking is reduced. And if we plant in layers, many plants can share the same space. — snowflakes can push through violas and forget-me-nots, which carpet the ground beneath a marguerite daisy, itself nestled in the arms of a buddleia.

With this sort of conniving, a Posy Garden can become an enormous living bouquet in its own right — a cloud of colours melting into each other.

Plan for a Posy Garden

The Posy Garden is an oval-shaped island bed, perhaps in the centre of a lawn, at least 8 metres (26 ft) long and 6 metres (20 ft) wide. As you walk along the narrow paths, weaving in and around the plantings, the sensation is of being in a sea of flowers, where blooms and foliage lap at your legs as you pass.

The garden follows a series of colour schemes. Either side of the entrance path is a blue and yellow theme. This blends into pale pink, and then, in the far reaches of the garden, a white, silver and blue theme culminates in a timber tripod entwined with a climbing 'Iceberg' rose, atop a silvery pool of catmint (*Nepeta* x *faassenii*). This tripod, the gar-den's only vertical accent, marks the furthest point from the entry and acts as a lure for wanderers.

At the heart of the garden, vibrant and glowing, are sun-flowers, the Posy Garden's centrepiece. These are surrounded by marigolds, rich pink, deep red and golden yellow kangaroo paws (*Anigozanthos*), and an explosion of dahlias. The peachy tones of *Achillea* 'Salmon Beauty' join in with this bright, carnival atmosphere, but also sing in harmony with the pink tones across the path from Japanese windflower, *Salvia coccinea* and 'The Fairy' rose.

The four remaining petal-shaped gardens are planted with bulbs and a few low-growing companions: fragrant freesias with violets; *Nerine* and agapanthus; snowflakes with parsley; and scented jonquils with Chinese forget-me-not (*Cyno-glossum amabile*).

This garden is designed for a sunny location, but many of the plants shown will also grow in shade or part shade, including silver and gold helichrysum, Japanese windflower, peppermint-scented geranium, daphne, golden marjoram, sweet violets, pansies, variegated applemint, Chinese forget-me-not and parsley. In deep shade plant hellebore, nasturtium, arum lily, ferns and ivy.

If you have more space to devote to the Posy Garden, lay a path around the perimeter and plant shrubs — such as camellia, roses, buddleia, Geraldton wax, hibiscus, mock orange, winter jasmine, winter sweet, lemon-scented verbena (*Aloysia triphylla*), and clematis for float bowls. You may like to choose some flowers to match your interior furnishings.

The Posy Garden is good to share with friends. Give them a pair of secateurs and a basket and invite them to walk the paths and pick their own country bunch. Each person will interpret the flowers and foliage in a new way, providing fresh inspiration for your own arrangements.

A Smaller Posy Garden

The smaller the Posy Garden, the more chaotic and crowded it can afford to be. All the plants in the large plan are a manageable size, so select your favourites, squeeze them in, then make serpentine paths throughout the garden so all plants are within easy picking distance.

To bring a sense of order to the plan, give the garden a pristine edge of tightly clipped rosemary, santolina, box (*Buxus*) or small-leafed honeysuckle (*Lonicera nitida*). Or, if you have time and patience, turn the garden into a basket of flowers by adding a wickerwork edge. To do this, encircle the garden with short sticks at regular 30-cm (12-in) intervals, then weave in and out with threads of willow, or vines such as jasmine or honeysuckle, stripped of their leaves.

A Tiny Posy Garden

In a tiny garden, make a rug of posy flowers using smaller-growing plants, such as flannel flower, eryngium, sweet violets, campanula, scabious, pansies, nasturtiums, forget-me-not, cottage pinks (*Dianthus plumarius*) and a changing display of small annual plants. Embroider them, one next to the other, into a seamless carpet, snipping them into shape as they grow. If the garden is too wide for you to reach flowers at its centre, tuck a tiny path or a series of stepping stones beneath the flowers and foliage.

A seasonally changing display of potted plants is an eye-catching approach for a terrace or balcony Posy Garden. Among the best annuals are sunflowers, cosmos, love-in-a-mist and lupins. These can be supported by mainstays such as lavender, catmint, *Anthemis tinctoria* 'E.C. Buxton' and marguerite daisies, and foliage plants such as bronze fennel, silver helichrysum, *Artemisia* 'Powis Castle' and variegated applemint. If there is room, add potted bulbs and a few smaller-growing shrubs, such as daphne and 'The Fairy' rose; also, dwarf varieties of kangaroo paw such as yellow-flowering *Anigozanthos manglesii* 'Bush Dawn'. For jewel-like posies, fill window boxes and hanging baskets with topaz, ruby, sapphire and turquoise by choosing pansies, marigolds, nasturtiums and zinnias in brilliant hues.

Chapter 14

The Maze Garden

Once seen, a maze cannot be ignored.
It draws you in like a magnet,
then proceeds to puzzle, infuriate and delight in turn
until its goal is reached.

John Spencer-Churchill, 11th Duke of Marlborough

'What is the attraction of mazes,' asks the Duke of Marlborough in the preface to *Labyrinth: Solving the Riddle of the Maze* by Adrian Fisher, 'and why have they endured and recreated themselves, phoenix-like, from century to century in all parts of the world?'

Perhaps it is because entering a maze is like entering another world — simple and structured, yet full of complexity. Through head-high hedges, you take a journey of twists, turns and puzzlement. You tread narrow paths surrounded by green, delighting in the disorientation and the thrill of imagined danger — perhaps you will be lost inside this new world forever, unable to escape.

Considering their great magnetism, not to mention the fun to be had, it is a shame mazes are so rarely seen beyond the grand gardens of country houses; especially when mazes come in shapes and forms to fit almost any outdoor space.

For many people, the ultimate is the one that requires the most space — the hedge maze. A dense wall of green, broken only by an entrance, is always enticing, but when that entrance leads to even more green walls and a labyrinth of paths, it is irresistible. Here is a place where you can truly lose yourself.

For this sort of maze you need a larger than average-sized backyard with a wide, open space. A sunny area is best, away from tall trees which will compete for water and nutrition.

Choose attractive, densely leafed evergreen hedging plants that respond well to close trimming. Those which can be clipped to a width of 60 cm (2 ft) are ideal. Conifers, such as yew (*Taxus baccata*) and Monterey cypress (*Cupressus macrocarpa* 'Lambertiana Aurea'), are traditional and reliable favourites. In warm areas, hedges can be fashioned from lillypilly (*Acmena smithii*) or orange-scented jessamine (*Murraya paniculata*). Camellias are a good choice for a maze that has a shaded position. *Camellia sasanqua* tolerates both sun and shade.

Before setting out to make a hedge maze there are a few important considerations. First, there's the expense. Hedging plants can be costly, especially in the quantities needed for most mazes. Be sure to cost the project before the ground is dug. Consider, too, the ongoing maintenance. All hedges require regular feeding, watering and pruning. Do you have time to do this yourself? If not, can you afford to pay someone to do it for you? If the answer to these questions is no, or your budget is small, you may need to consider other options.

You could, for example, replace hedges with trellis panels woven with fragrant climbers and espaliered fruit trees, creating pathways where scent hovers on warm air.

Another alternative is to separate the paths with fragrant festoons. Simply sink poles into the ground at regular intervals and string thick rope between them. Plant vines, such as climbing roses, at the base of each pole and train them along the ropes to set a colourful and festive mood. In fact, a rope maze in its most simple form — made of stakes and string — is an ideal 'trial stage' for a maze, especially one which involves a puzzle.

There is a certain art to the puzzle maze. Its level of difficulty should lie in that magical zone between easy and arduous. It has been said that the perfect puzzle maze is solved just minutes before people begin to lose interest … or begin to panic. Most theme park mazes take around 15 minutes to solve, while those at stately homes and country estates tend to take around 30 minutes. The most satisfying backyard maze probably has a solving time

somewhere in between. Test it out on your family, friends and neighbours — but be sure to do so before construction.

Another factor to consider with any maze, but particularly one involving a puzzle, is a reward to mark the goal. A seat, fountain, sculpture, or, in the largest of gardens, a pavilion, makes the journey seem all the more worthwhile.

If you have a passion for puzzles — and unlimited space with a budget to match — consider a complex state-of-the-art maze. Three-dimensional mazes, for instance, incorporate bridges and underpasses, while interactive mazes have moving parts such as swinging gates, so the puzzle is ever-changing.

But mazes need not involve a puzzle. In fact the puzzle maze is a relative newcomer, appearing first in the sixteenth century. Before this, mazes were of a 'unicursal design' — they had a single, twisting, turning path that led to an inevitable end point, without the disappointment and rejection of dead ends.

Unicursal mazes have a simple, becalming beauty. Walking them generates a restful optimism — you can enjoy the disorientation for its own sake, knowing that each step takes you closer to your goal.

Generally speaking, unicursal mazes are more suitable than puzzle mazes for small and average-sized gardens because every path is used and necessary. So, for anyone with a wanderlust of the garden variety, this makes the most of available space. And games are still possible. Centuries ago in Europe, unicursal mazes were often the scene of running races. In Britain, for example, such races were part of village life, and mazes were often found on the common, green or fairground. These were usually turf mazes — a convoluted path in the lawn with no visual barriers at all. Though, through constant use, the path gradually became a deep rut.

ORANGE-SCENTED JESSAMINE

LILLYPILLY

YEW

ABELIA

MONTEREY CYPRESS

Camellia sasanqua

Any one of the species indicated can be used
to fashion this unicursal hedge maze which
has a secluded sitting area at its centre.

Turf mazes are an excellent option for tight spaces … and tight budgets. A little planning means they are relatively low-maintenance as well. A brick edge for wheels to run along makes mowing a quick and easy operation — and just another excuse to walk the maze.

An interesting variation has grass paths with water channels running between them. Somehow this hints at the excitement of walking along a cliff face with a ravine either side. On warm days you can kick off your shoes, plunge in and wade through water instead.

Another option, for which you need no garden at all, is a pavement maze. In this case 'paths' and 'hedges' are represented in two-dimensions using any sort of paving material including bricks, tiles, pebbles or mosaic tiles. The paths need only be as wide as a shoe, so even an elaborate maze can be relatively compact. The design can be free-form or structured — such as the wonderful octagonal pavement mazes of some Gothic churches. And because of the ease of escape, they can be as complex and puzzling as you dare. Aim for a design that you will never learn by rote — one that stumps you and your friends time and again.

When designing pavement mazes, and others as well, search out a good reference book on the subject. Here you will find a wealth of inspiration, and detailed plans that

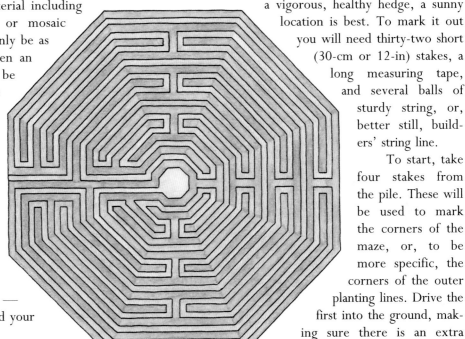

This design for an octagonal pavement maze is typical of those found in medieval Christian churches.

may help you adapt or recreate some of the world's great mazes in miniature.

Unfortunately, even a quick skim through such books will probably leave you swimming in ideas and wishing you had an acreage. If so, look around your local area. A maze could make an ideal community project for a neglected or under-used park.

Plan for a Maze Garden

The unicursal hedge maze shown opposite and on page 94 (adapted from Barbara Gallup and Deborah Reich's maze in *The Complete Book of Topiary*) requires an area of 12 square metres (40 sq ft). For a vigorous, healthy hedge, a sunny location is best. To mark it out you will need thirty-two short (30-cm or 12-in) stakes, a long measuring tape, and several balls of sturdy string, or, better still, builders' string line.

To start, take four stakes from the pile. These will be used to mark the corners of the maze, or, to be more specific, the corners of the outer planting lines. Drive the first into the ground, making sure there is an extra 30 cm (12 in) beyond the stake for the mature hedge. Measure out 11.5 metres (38 ft) from this stake to mark the second corner. Then do the same for the third and fourth

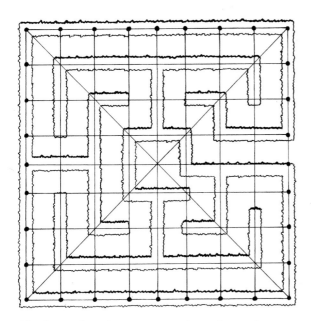

This diagram shows the peg positions and string lines used to create the large Maze Garden. It also serves as a useful guide for creating smaller mazes. Follow the directions for the large plan, reducing the space between stakes to a minimum of 60 cm (2 ft). Smaller mazes may be planted with knee-high hedges, or a labyrinth of flowers.

corner. Check that all four sides are exactly 11.5 metres (38 ft) long. Measure the diagonals. If they are equal in length, right angles have been formed; if not, adjust the corner posts. You have now established the corner posts from which all the measurements will be taken. Stretch string between them.

Take six more stakes and return to the first corner post. Measure 1.5 metres (4½ ft) from the corner stake along one of the sides and set out a stake. Set out another 1.5 metres (4½ ft) from this one, and finally another, again 1.5 metres (4½ ft) away. You should now have four evenly spaced stakes, including the corner post. Now set out three more stakes in the same way on the other side of the first corner post.

Repeat this process for the other three corner posts, then make a grid of string lines as shown in the diagram on the left. With the four remaining stakes, mark the halfway point on each side, by measuring 5.75 metres (19 ft) along each side. Connect these points with two lengths of string to form a cross. Now mark the diagonal lines by stretching string from one corner to another. The intersection of the two diagonal and two halfway strings marks the centre point of the maze.

You now have the basic guidelines needed to mark out the maze. Following the diagram, mark out the planting lines for hedges on the ground using spray paint. You will find the planting lines are directly below string lines, except in the case of the hedge that runs along the left-hand side of the entrance corridor, which, as the diagram shows, is 30 cm (12 in) to the left of the central string line.

When you are sure the pattern is correct, the stakes and string can be removed and the garden beds dug. Make the garden beds 60 cm (2 ft) wide. Note that the painted line marks the centre of the garden beds. Once the beds are dug, the space remaining for paths should be 90 cm (3 ft) wide.

As already mentioned, conifers such as yew and some cypress are ideal for hedge mazes, given the right climate. Consult a local nursery or qualified landscape gardener for advice on the most suitable species for your soil and climate.

Consider bark chips for the paths. They are relatively inexpensive, provide a pleasant softness underfoot and have great benefits for the hedge — they preserve soil moisture, gradually break down into plant food and provide the root system with protection from trampling.

The goal at the centre of this maze is around 2 metres (over 6 ft) square — ideal for a seat to relax on at the end of the journey. Alternatively, it makes a wonderfully secluded bathing area (see Chapter 11).

A Smaller Maze Garden

By shrinking the garden beds and paths of the large plan, the same maze design can be reduced to fit an area less than 5 square metres (15 sq ft). Follow the instructions for the larger plan, but this time measure out sides 4.6 metres (13 ft 10 in) long, and space the stakes at 60-cm (2-ft) intervals from the corner posts.

This design allows around 30 cm (12 in) for garden beds, and the same for paths. Even in this compact state the maze has 40 metres (120 ft) of garden beds. They are narrow, however, and will not accommodate large hedging plants, so, for a head-high maze, trellis panels planted with climbers or espaliered trees or shrubs are the best option. If you are captivated by hedges, try smaller-growers such as santolina, box (*Buxus*), small-leafed honey-suckle (*Lonicera nitida*), and compact varieties of *Hebe,* such as *Hebe diosmifolia* and *H. buxifolia.*

Alternatively, plant a maze of earthly delights. In fact, a maze is an ideal showcase for many of the smaller plants described in the previous chapters, such as those in the Fragrant Garden, Touching Garden, Butterfly Garden, Tea Garden and Posy Garden. A Tasting Garden maze could include berries, and may-be even a rescue party — as William Lawson pointed out in his seven-teenth-century classic *A New Orchard and Garden*:

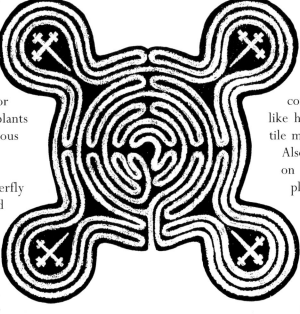

This turf maze, called Robin Hood's Race, once existed near Sneinton, Nottinghamshire, in the UK.

'Mazes may perhaps take your friend wandering in the gathering of berries until he cannot recover himself without your help.'

A Tiny Maze Garden

Pavement mazes which use bricks, tiles, pavers or pebbles, as already described, are an elegant option for balconies and paved areas. But, if what you really long for is a 'green maze', why not combine these hard surfaces with trails of fragrant mat-forming plants such as Corsican mint, wild thyme or lawn chamomile. These can be the maze's tiny barefoot paths.

A pavement maze need not be a permanent fixture, either. An occasional maze is also possible — a giant jigsaw, taken out and put away as desired. A durable material for this portable puzzle is carpet tiles, cut into various sizes. Of course, making a portable maze involves some work, but no more than it takes to construct a hedge maze. Un-like hedges, however, a carpet-tile maze needs no maintenance. Also, by numbering each piece on the back according to placement, setting up is easy.

The smallest space can have dozens of 'gaze mazes' — traced with a finger, the paths can be as tiny as your small-est finger. The pattern can be engraved in wood or clay, or laid as a mosaic on walls and floors.

Landscaping Your Garden

Chapter 15

Horizontal Elements

Paths

Paths are an exciting opportunity to lead people wherever you want them to go; to take them on a journey. When a path is designed for pleasure, each step brings new delights — an overhanging rose to sink your nose into, fruit to pick and eat, or a chance meeting with a bird or lizard. Yet the most successful path will make all this wizardry look almost accidental, as if the whole garden has sprouted from a heavenly spring of pleasure which runs deep beneath its soil.

The 'foundations' of the best paths are grounded, first of all, in practical considerations. This is especially true of paths which are used every day. These should be wide, firm, flowing, well-defined and comfortable for people of all ages and degrees of mobility. The route should always be convenient — sometimes a worn track in the lawn is a good guide.

The best width for a path depends on how you want to use it: for two people to comfortably walk side by side, it should be 120 to 150 cm (4 to 5 ft) wide; one person is comfortable on a path around 90 cm (3 ft) wide; while less frequently used paths can be quite narrow at around 40 to 60 cm (16 in to 2 ft) wide.

There are a vast number of surfaces to choose from and each brings its own texture, colour, mood and feel. Bricks, pavers, stone, concrete pebbles, sawn logs, timber decking, railway sleepers and bark chips are just some of the options and they can be used in patterns and combinations which are limited only by the imagination.

You may like to combine these materials with plantings. Small gaps here and there can be filled with fragrant cushions such as thyme, chamomile, golden marjoram and Corsican mint which spill over and soften hard edges, and release their scent when stepped upon. Or, rather than just a few plants, you could have many — for instance, a river of swirling fragrance and colour through which stepping stones may meander.

Even if you decide not to incorporate plants into the path, you can still have fun with the plantings either side. In fact, a path is a wonderful opportunity to stage-manage various experiences along its length in the way of scents, tastes and textures. In Victorian England, scented geraniums were planted alongside the path so the long skirts of perambulating ladies could brush the foliage and release the scent. Other plants which will leave fragrant clouds in your wake are rosemary, lavender, pineapple sage, thyme and fennel. Include fragrant flowers, too, so you can drink in their scent as you pass, for example, daphne, heliotrope, gardenia, freesias and roses.

The close quarters of a path are also a perfect opportunity for touch sensations from plants such as fennel, *Artemisia* 'Powis Castle', lamb's ear (*Stachys byzantina*), dusty miller (*Centaurea cineraria*), and fountain grass (*Pennisetum alopecuroides*); and it provides easy-pickings from blueberry, strawberry, parsley, cherry tomatoes, and nasturtiums and freesias for the sip of honey at the base of their flowers.

Landscape design emphasises that a path should always lead somewhere, and it is true that a path without purpose is full of disappointment. If it is a cul-de-sac, always offer the wanderer something at its end — a seat, gazebo or sundial, for instance.

One of the most satisfying paths is one which takes you back to where you began without retracing your steps — a 'looped' path. When you walk a looped path, especially one where there are things to do and see along the way, you feel you've been somewhere and accomplished something; it is a miniature adventure. One of the best things about looped paths is that you get two paths in one because the experience is slightly different when walked in the opposite direction.

The looped path is used in many garden plans throughout this book. In most, it is shown as a circular path, but it need not be so formal. Loops can be made to fit the shape and mood of the garden; they may twist and turn and be quite elongated in shape; they may also be big or small.

In the smallest garden a tiny looped path is created using a centrepiece. The path might loop around a fountain, pool, birdbath, or a table with chairs; or plants may be used — such as a fragrant standard, or a circular 'rug' woven with flowers.

In large gardens loops can lead off the main path and return. The Australian garden designer Ellis Stones incorporated this idea into many of his designs. He called these trails, which were often half-hidden by foliage, 'sneak tracks'. Little touches like this add magic to a garden, and there are other ways, too.

A path which includes a bridge suggests thrills and adventure, and perhaps even danger. Of course the ultimate bridge would be a grand affair over a swirling torrent of water, but neither water nor height is necessary. Even when the 'bridge' is barely 30 cm (1 ft) from solid ground, the heart dances on crossing. So often in the garden the power of suggestion is almost as powerful as the real thing. A mock bridge, such as this, is an excellent design solution for a path which passes through a boggy spot or a dip in the terrain. In its simplest form it is a short section of timber decking. A more substantial 'bridge', traversing a small gully, for instance, can be bordered by a dry stone wall on either side.

Another path experience guaranteed to delight is one which leads by stepping stones over a pond. You can arrange the stepping stones so they seem to 'float' on the water's surface. This gives a sense of walking on water, or lily pads. Garden-makers interested in generating thrills may prefer to use tall stepping stones, or sawn logs, which seem to tower above the water.

Steps
....

Strange though it may seem, steps tend to have voices. As soon as you see them, they invite you to use them. If they lead somewhere mysterious — somewhere not quite seen — our curiosity is sparked and the invitation becomes irresistible. Standing at the top or the bottom of a staircase, another voice is heard. A steep, narrow flight of steps says 'hurry up', while one with a gentle gradient, plenty of room for our feet and a generous width, says 'take your time, savour the moment'. It is the latter voice that we usually want to encourage in our gardens.

Landscape professionals have developed a formula for the proportions of steps. The riser (R) is the height of each step, and the tread (T) is the width where the foot is placed. To obtain a comfortable proportion for your steps, you'll need to end up with a total measurement of between 650 and 680 mm (26 and 27 in). The formula is (R x 2) + T = 650 to 680 mm (e.g. if your riser is 150 mm, multiply by 2 to give 300 mm; take this figure away from the total, and you will have the ideal measurement for the tread: 350 to 380 mm). Or you can work out the formula in reverse: 650 to 680 mm − (T ÷ 2) = R. This is an excellent and trusted guide which you may like to back up with your own observations. Carry a tape measure and, when you find steps which have a restful and welcoming voice, take note of the riser and tread.

Whatever the measurement of the riser and tread, they should be uniform throughout the flight. This is essential for steps which are used every day. People expect a predictable rhythm and may fall if the step is not where their foot expects it to be. However, there are exceptions to this rule. Steps which are used less frequently — stone steps in a wild or informal part of the garden, for instance — may vary with the natural terrain.

Consider the lateral width of the steps, as well. Make them at least as wide as the paths which meet them. If you want to be able to walk two people abreast the steps must be at least 1.5 metres (5 ft) wide. Wide staircases are always the most restful and enticing. One of the most inviting designs is a series of concentric semicircles, each with a wide tread and shallow riser. A circular landing at the top adds to its graciousness.

There are a number of ways of using a set of steps. If the path has enough lateral width, a collection of potted scented geraniums may be lined up, one to a step, to stroke as you pass. Where the steps are set into a wall, plants can spill over the edge from the garden, or pots, above. Plants which can be used for this purpose include prostrate rosemary, *Gardenia augusta* 'Radicans' and butterfly-attracting *Lantana montevidensis*.

An informal set of stairs looks beautiful when the boundary between the steps and the garden is blurred by the spill and tumble of soft, mounding plants. To encourage this effect, leave small random soil pockets at the sides of some treads and pop in any of the fragrant hummocks that are so useful for paths.

Cracks and gaps in paths and paving are the perfect home for all those lovely plants which run wild in open spaces. Here, their forthright habits are just what is needed to elbow weeds out of the way.

Paving

Paved areas, large and small, are ideal spaces to be furnished with a seat or tables and chairs — in fact, anywhere that a solid, even surface is needed.

Choose a paving material to suit your house and the surrounding garden. Stone and bricks are amongst the most pleasant surfaces to use, and each develops a patina of weathered hues, mosses and lichens. Rather than deteriorating, these surfaces improve and blend with the garden a little more every year.

If the area is not shaded by trees, be sure to add protection from the sun. The cover you choose will depend on the mood and size of the space. A large market umbrella may be all you need, or you could add an arbour or a pergola with a deciduous climber to let in the winter sun and shade you from summer's harsh rays. Other suggestions can be found in Chapter 16.

The beds which surround a paved area can be one of the most exciting parts of the garden. Here, more than anywhere else, your clever use of plants will enhance the enjoyment of the space for everyone who uses it; here, too, you have a captive audience. In fact, the surrounding gardens are an ideal setting for many of the Pleasure Gardens discussed in this book. Those which deserve special consideration include the Fragrant, Tasting, Night, Tea, Posy, Reading, Butterfly, Bird and Wildlife Gardens. Each of these could be used by themselves or in combination. With thoughtful plant selection and the aid of the Key Guide in Chapter 17, even a relatively small garden should be able to include at least a few plants from each.

In the clamour for space, why not include small plants in the paving itself? Paving cracks or gaps can be filled with mat-forming plants such as lawn chamomile, wild thyme and Corsican mint. If it is a very large sunny area with plenty of room to manoeuvre, consider including a few 'step-over' gardens around the perimeter with slightly taller-growing plants like violets, pansies, applemint, prostrate rosemary, scented geranium, sweet alyssum, golden marjoram, pinks (*Dianthus*) and *Brachyscome multifida*.

Lawns

A lawn can be one of the garden's most pleasurable spaces — it offers the possibility of gatherings, picnics, and a comfortable place to snooze, and it is unsurpassed as a surface for games — not many other plants let you tread all over them.

Recently, however, lawns have received bad press. The most common criticism is the amount of mowing, weeding, feeding and watering they require. Ideally, the time you spend on a lawn should be relative to the amount of fun and enjoyment it gives in return. If is used only for games or a place to spread a rug, there is no real need to pamper it. If you choose a variety to suit your climate and rainfall, mowing may be the only necessary care. It may brown a little during dry times, but, rest assured, it will almost always return to green after heavy rains.

A luxurious, fine-textured sward, on the other hand, requires plenty of work to keep it pristine. But if it adds immeasurably to your enjoyment of the garden, it may well be worth every effort you bestow on it, and it is possible you may even *enjoy* nurturing it.

Most gardens have much more lawn than they need. If this applies to your garden, rather than give up your lawn altogether, perhaps you could reduce it to a useful size. Be sure, though, to err on the side of too much, rather than too little. It is easy enough to claim lawn for garden beds if you need to later.

Choosing a grass variety needs great care. It is important to choose a lawn which suits you and your garden. The first consideration should be the growing conditions — your climate, the soil, and the amount of sun and shade the area receives. Then consider the use or uses the lawn will have. What feel and appearance do you want? Is it simply a luscious surface for lying on, or will it need to withstand constant foot traffic and games? The final consideration is maintenance. How much water are you willing to expend, and how often do you want to mow? If you have the answers to these questions, a good turf supplier or grass seed merchant should be able to lead you to a grass to suit your needs.

Consider a fragrant herb lawn, too, especially if you want to use it for sitting and lying, and the sheer pleasure of kicking off your shoes and feeling plants underfoot. Pennyroyal and Corsican mint are best for moist shady areas, and both will take light foot traffic. For sunny, well-drained areas, thyme and chamomile are the most commonly planted herb lawns.

Rudyard Kipling described thyme's fragrance as being 'like the perfume of the dawn of Paradise'. To fully experience this glorious scent the leaves must be touched and the most rapturous way of doing so is to lie or sit on a thyme lawn. There are many species of thyme, but the one to use for this purpose is wild, or creeping thyme (*Thymus serpyllum*). Within this species there are dozens of varieties to choose from, each a little different in flower or foliage colour, and often in leaf texture, as well.

This palette of colour and texture can be used to create a limitless array of exciting patterns and patchworks. Vita Sackville-West described her thyme lawn 'while densely flowering in purple and red' as looking like 'a Persian carpet laid flat on the ground out of doors'. Her thyme lawns at Sissinghurst Castle in Kent, England, are still maintained today and are amongst the most famous and celebrated in the world.

Wild thyme spreads by setting out runners as it grows. If it has a sunny, well-drained position it will spread happily and relatively quickly.

The chamomile lawn dates back to Tudor times, and is perhaps the most romantic of all fragrant lawns. A number of plants go by the name of chamomile including German chamomile (*Matricaria recutita*) and dyer's chamomile (*Anthemis tinctoria*), but the one to use for lawns is, not surprisingly, referred to as lawn chamomile (*Chamaemelum nobile*). To confuse the issue further, lawn chamomile itself has a couple of different cultivars, as well as the species itself. Of these, the one most commonly used for lawns is 'Treneague', a cultivar with a low-growing, tidy habit. If, however, you dream of sipping chamomile tea on the lawn that produced it, you will have to settle for the less compact effect of the species or the pretty double-flowering cultivar 'Flore Pleno', because 'Treneague' is non-flowering. Apart from the fragrance, chamomile has a lovely feel to it — soft and ferny with a springy sensation underfoot.

A chamomile lawn takes a little more time to prepare and plant than a thyme lawn. Begin by raking the soil with compost, a little manure and some coarse sand or fine grit. The most economical way to plant a chamomile lawn is to divide the contents of each pot bought at the nursery into little pieces which have their own roots; these are called rooted offsets. Do this gently, teasing out pieces with your fingers. Plant these offsets about 15 cm (6 in) apart. Weed regularly until the lawn is established, then an occasional mow on a high blade setting or a clip with hedging shears, and a light feed will keep it healthy. Chamomile lawns, like thyme lawns, must have a sunny, well-drained position. If you cannot provide these conditions it is best not to attempt one.

Chapter 16

Vertical Elements

Walls and Fences

Every bare wall and fence is a blank canvas waiting to be brought to life. As you layer delights into your garden, and become aware of preserving your ground space, look to your walls and fences. With only a little loss of ground space, you could create an *upright* Pleasure Garden.

Climbing plants are often the easiest way to clothe a wall or fence. Once they are in the ground or placed in a pot, most need only a little training and clipping, and for anyone with a creative urge, the field of walls and climbers offers plenty of scope for exploration. Without too much effort plants can be directed into two-dimensional shapes and patterns, or woven into a continuous wall of foliage.

For a curtain of flower-spangled foliage, train a climber to cover the entire wall. This may be achieved with a single vine, or a number intertwined. Much fun can be had mixing two or more plants together. For instance, you may plan for a succession of fragrance and fruit from one end of the year to the other; or, alternatively, a crescendo with plants which 'perform' at the same time of the year.

To concentrate fragrance where it will be enjoyed, both inside and outside the house, frame windows and doors with a neat band of foliage and flower. This elegant idea is also very clever — fragrance sweeps into the house on breezes, and it can be breathed in as you open windows, or enter and leave the house. Wisteria, roses, jasmines and honeysuckles are some scented climbers which can be used to achieve this effect.

There is a climber to suit every pleasure scheme, but three deserve special mention because of the great variety of delights they bring. Poet's jasmine (*Jasminum officinale*) has fragrant night-shining flowers which can be brewed to make tea, added to the bath, or used as an accompaniment in posies. Climbing 'Iceberg' rose also has fragrant white blooms for Night Gardens, and petals to add to a bath, or a teapot for rose petal tea. Passionfruit vine has delicious fruit, fascinating white flowers which catch the moonlight, and the leaves and flowers bring butterflies and their caterpillars. These three plants are all sun-lovers, although 'Iceberg' roses also tolerate shade.

Selecting pleasurable climbers for shaded walls is a greater challenge than for walls which bask in the sun. Two proven favourites are fragrant, butterfly-attracting Chinese star jasmine (*Trachelospermum jasminoides*), and Australian native kangaroo vine (*Cissus antarctica*) for birds and other fruit-eating wildlife. Vines which bring fragrance to shady walls and fences include akebia, *Clematis montana*, the white sweet-scented climbing rose 'Madame Alfred Carrière' and the pink-flowering rambler 'New Dawn'.

Before you plant a climber, think about maintenance on the wall behind. This is especially important when growing plants on painted walls. Being forced to cut down a healthy plant in its prime can be heart-breaking. You will certainly thank yourself if you have planned for this in advance. Trellis panels with a series of hinges along their bottom edge and screws along the top can be laid flat on the ground when it comes time to paint. If the vine is grown in a pot, the trellis can be completely unscrewed and the whole effect moved somewhere else.

A delicious way to cover a wall is with espaliered fruit trees. This plant-training technique, which encourages plants to grow on a flat plane, is decorative, uses a minimum of garden space and often encourages heavy cropping. The best fruit trees for sunny walls include apples, pears, peaches, apricots, nectarines, oranges, lemons, figs and almonds. Shady walls can be decorated with the fruits of morello cherries, gooseberries and red currants. Your local specialist fruit nursery or department of agriculture should be able to tell you which of these are suitable for your climate, how much wall space you need and whether a second plant is necessary for cross-pollination. It is also wise to consult a good book on the subject.

'Wall gardening' is perhaps at its most exciting when it offers as many experiences as the open garden and all within easy reach of the hand … and nose. Dozens of plants can be squeezed onto a relatively small wall using wall pots, half baskets, window boxes and hanging baskets. Why not choose a mix of the smaller plants recommended for container growing in previous chapters and in the Key Guide of the Pleasure Plant Index? Then you and a friend can 'wander' your wall — picking strawberries, posy flowers, fresh leaves for salads and herbs for tea. Or you can sit back and await visits from birds, bees, butterflies or night-flying moths. In fact, a sturdy built-in seat along the length of the wall serves double duty by helping you to reach higher, and thus increasing your gardening space.

While you are busy pondering your existing walls, take time to think about adding more walls or fences to your garden. Even quite small gardens benefit from added privacy and screening, and the fences or walls may make the garden more useable and enticing, creating a series of compartments or rooms. For instance, a well-positioned wall or fence can create a retreat protected from winds for basking in the sun, or, on its other side, a shelter in cool moist shade.

Whenever you add a wall to your garden, make the world beyond enticing by offering glimpses through open 'doorways' and perhaps even 'windows'. These little touches allude to interior spaces and make us feel at home and, when covered in green, they leave us in no doubt that this garden is also a place of adventure.

Arches and Tunnels

Arches and tunnels covered with leafy branches and flowers or fruit help to maximise our enjoyment of a garden using a minimum of space.

When it is well-placed, an arch makes a welcoming and enticing doorway. One of the best positions for an arch, especially in a small garden, is over the entry path, as soon as one steps into the garden. It is also an enchanting way to signal the passage to a separate garden room or an area with its own distinctive mood. Arches can be purchased ready-made from most nurseries and garden centres, or you can build one yourself using materials such as timber, trellis or metal piping.

Whereas arches act as doorways in the garden, tunnels act as hallways, so they are most satisfying when they lead somewhere. The most enticing tunnels have a reward at the end such as a fine seat, fountain or sculpture which shines in the sunlight beyond the tunnel's final arc. For wanderers, green tunnels are pure delight. They offer a chance to enjoy the dappled sun or moonlight, feeling nestled in foliage and protected from wind and dust.

Tunnels are usually constructed with a frame of timber or metal but almost any material can be used — as long as it is strong enough to support the weight of the chosen plants. A simple, yet effective, design is similar to a free-standing pergola, with extra beams and wires along the sides on which to train foliage for walls.

Two of the best plants for tunnels are grape and wisteria. Each is wonderful from below — grape with its juicy clusters of fruit, and wisteria with its dangling racemes of mauve or white flowers. And both conveniently throw off their luscious cloak of leaves to let the sun stream in through the colder months. The wonderful feel of their fresh new foliage and their gnarled and twisted trunks further add to their appeal. Both, however, need strong support.

Tunnels may also be quite open and airy — a series of evenly spaced, free-standing arches, technically referred to as an arcade. The world's most admired example is probably Monet's Grand Allée in Giverny in France. This is a wonderful way to promenade amongst your favourite fragrant climbers. A different vine may be trained on each frame, or two may be planted at either end to meet and meld into a tapestry of colour. If you have a large garden, an arcade is guaranteed to lure wanderers from one area to another.

Any of the climbers recommended for walls will work equally well here, but it is important to match the vigour of the vine to the size of the arch. Monet chose climbing and rambling roses for his wide-span arches and some of the best roses for this purpose include 'Crepuscule', 'Albertine', 'New Dawn', 'Iceberg', 'Zephirine Drouhin', 'Kathleen Harrop' and 'Madame Alfred Carrière'. Pre-fabricated arches in large sizes may be difficult to find, but a local metal fabricator should be able to custom-make frames to your own design and specifications.

Pergolas

A pergola is a simple, easily-built structure which provides the garden with a venue for outdoor living. It may be little more than four columns with supporting beams overhead, but it can add immeasurably to your leisure time and lure you, your family and friends into the fresh air, and the sounds and scents of the garden at every opportunity.

Perhaps the best thing about a pergola is its versatility. It accommodates all forms of relaxation from reading books and newspapers, to alfresco dining and entertaining, and if you have outdoor cooking facilities it can become an outdoor kitchen as well.

A sunny, wind-protected position ensures the pergola will be used for many months of the year, and perhaps even year-round in mild climates. For extra comfort, deciduous plants provide built-in, natural, climate control. The best choices are the same as those for a tunnel — grape and wisteria. Wisteria grows in a wide range of soils and climates, but fruiting grapes are more particular. To find out if grapes can be grown successfully in your area, contact a nursery which specialises in fruit, or your local department of agriculture. Be sure to ask which varieties are the tastiest and easiest to grow.

Arbours

A number of other garden structures, as well as the pergola, help to ensure the garden is the setting for gracious, comfortable outdoor living.

The simplest and most compact of these is an arbour — a cosy place just big enough for one or two people or a peaceful nook for reading or resting. Sometimes referred to as a bower, an arbour is at its romantic best when it is swathed in fragrant climbers, and tucked into the garden — somewhere it may be happened upon when wandering. Traditionally, an arbour was made by planting supple-stemmed trees or shrubs on three sides, often surrounding a seat. The main stems

were plaited overhead to form a roof, and side branches were interlaced to make walls. These days, an arbour is usually a simple timber construction woven with climbers. This leafy camouflage also makes it an excellent hide for wildlife watching.

Other Vertical Features

Upright forms, such as tripods and poles, add visual interest to a garden, and allow us to squeeze vines into the smallest of spaces.

Tripods can be used in the garden or in pots to display the talents of almost any climber. In a garden they may be used as central features in garden beds, or in pairs to mark an entrance or a change of mood. When used in pots, tripods transform climbers into portable garden features. When the climber is most enjoyable, it can be placed in a strategic position near a path, window, gate or doorway. This allows you to showcase your region's most exquisitely perfumed perennial climbers, and create a changing display of annual vines. Tripods are available in a range of sizes, or you can make them yourself — using stakes or bamboo, for instance. Be sure the tripod's size matches the vigour of the vine.

Poles set into the ground are another simple, space-effective way to grow climbers, especially robust, vigorous vines which need stability and room to roam. A series of poles, with rope or chain swagged between them, makes a grand climbing frame, especially for fragrant roses. Different species and varieties can be planted at the base of each pole and intertwined with each other along the ropes or chain. This effect can be used to outline a garden room, or beside a path or driveway so the fragrance can be savoured as you pass.

Chapter 17

The Pleasure Plant Index

The Pleasure Plant Index is a guide to some of the world's most enjoyable, lifestyle-enhancing plants. Use it as a design tool to find out more about plants which fulfill your favourite fancies from the preceeding chapters. Apart from the delights they bring, each plant species has been selected for its beauty, superior adaptability and ease of growing.

Every plant in the Index can be enjoyed in three or more different ways. Many have seven or more different purposes or pleasures. Using these plants ensures that you get the most from your garden, regardless of its size. With the right choice, just three plants in a window box, for instance, may offer 20 means of enjoying them.

Start with the Key Guide. This summarises, in an easy-to-read table, the enormous, often hidden, talents of this elite group of plants. It also includes practical information that will help you to create a garden which is tailor-made to your climate and conditions.

When you have found the plants most suited to you and your garden, turn to the Descriptions section for a detailed profile of each plant. Here you will find information on colour, height, flowering season and growing information, as well as details on how to unleash its powers to please. A number of the plants will survive outside their preferred climate, too — especially many of the frost-tender plants. These can be used as conservatory plants, or annuals for just one single, joyful season. Some can even live a double life, as a garden plant in summer and a potted plant, under cover, in winter.

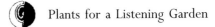
Key Guide

Plant size and type

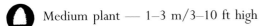 Small plant — up to 1 m/3 ft high

Medium plant — 1–3 m/3–10 ft high

Large plant — over 3 m/10 ft high

Climbing plant

Sun requirements

Grows in full sun

Grows in partly shaded conditions

Grows in full shade

Water needs

Low water needs

Medium to high drought tolerance

Frost-hardiness

Frost hardy to −7°C/20°F

Frost hardy to −12°C/10°F

Frost hardy to −18°C/0°F

Plants for Container-growing

Plants for Pots and Tubs

Plants for Hanging Baskets
and Window Boxes

Pleasure Garden Plants

Plants for a Listening Garden

Plants for a Fragrant Garden

Plants for a Touching Garden

Plants for a Tasting Garden

Plants for a Night Garden

Plants for a Bird Garden

Plants for a Butterfly Garden

Plants for a Wildlife Garden

Plants for a Bathing Garden

Plants for a Tea Garden

Plants for Posies and Flower Arrangements

Plants for a Maze Garden, Knot Garden
or Hedge

Water: The water needs ratings apply to established plants in soils with added compost and a deep layer of mulch.

Frost: The frost-hardiness ratings are intended as a guide only. Local microclimate, soil moisture, drainage, sunshine and winds will also affect plant survival. The ratings may refer to varieties or cultivars of the species. See Descriptions for more information.

Plant Name

Plant Name	1	2	3	4	5	6	7	8	9	10	11	12
1. *Abelia* x *grandiflora* Abelia #				●			●			●		●
2. *Acmena smithii* Lillypilly	●	●	●		●	●	●					
3. *Actinotus helianthi* Flannel flower	●				●		●					
4. *Aloysia triphylla* Lemon-scented verbena		●			●	●			●			
5. *Angelica archangelica* Angelica		●			●	●	●					
6. *Anigozanthos* species Kangaroo paw #	●	●			●				●			
7. *Argyranthemum frutescens* Marguerite daisy #	●	●			●	●		●				
8. *Artemisia* 'Powis Castle' #	●				●				●		●	
9. *Banksia ericifolia* Heath banksia			●		●				●	●		
10. *Brachyscome multifida* Cut-leaf daisy	●				●	●		●				
11. *Bracteantha bracteata* Everlasting daisy	●								●	●		
12. *Buddleja davidii* Buddleia #		●			●			●				
13. *Callistemon citrinus* cvs Crimson bottlebrush #		●			●				●	●		
14. *Chamaemelum nobile* Lawn chamomile	●				●							
15. *Citrus sinensis* Orange			●		●							
16. *Cymbopogon citratus* Lemongrass	●				●							
17. *Daphne odora* Daphne	●					●						●
18. *Dianthus plumarius* cvs Cottage pinks #	●				●	●	●					
19. *Eriostemon myoporoides* Waxflower		●			●				●	●		
20. *Foeniculum vulgare* Fennel	●				●				●			
21. *Freesia refracta* Freesia	●				●				●			
22. *Gardenia augusta* Gardenia	●	●			●							
23. *Grevillea* 'Robyn Gordon'		●			●				●			
24. *Grevillea rosmarinifolia* Rosemary grevillea #		●			●				●	●		
25. *Helianthus annuus* Sunflower	●	●			●		●					
26. *Helichrysum petiolare* Helichrysum #	●				●	●	●		●			
27. *Heliotropium arborescens* Heliotrope	●				●		●					
28. *Jasminum officinale* Poet's jasmine #			●		●	●	●					●
29. *Lavandula angustifolia* English lavender #	●				●				●			●
30. *Lavandula dentata* French lavender	●				●				●	●		
31. *Leptospermum petersonii* Lemon-scented tea tree			●		●	●	●					

This symbol indicates that the species or one of its varieties or cultivars has a Royal Horticultural Society Award of Merit.

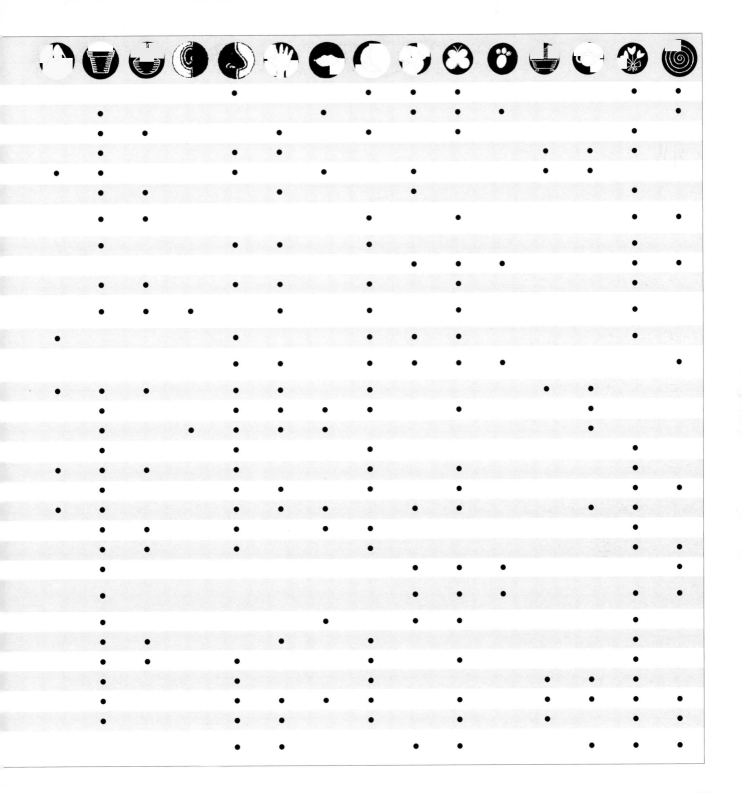

Plant Name	1	2	3	4	5	6	7	8	9	10	11
32. *Lobularia maritima* Sweet alyssum	●				●				●		
33. *Lunaria annua* Honesty #	●				●	●	●	●			
34. *Malus pumila* Apple	●	●	●		●			●			
35. *Mentha* x *piperita* Peppermint	●					●		●			
36. *Mentha suaveolens* 'Variegata' Applemint	●					●	●	●			
37. *Miscanthus sinensis* 'Zebrinus' Zebra grass #		●			●	●		●			
38. *Monarda didyma* Bergamot	●				●	●					
39. *Murraya paniculata* Orange-scented jessamine			●		●			●			
40. *Nepeta* x *faassenii* Catmint	●				●				●		
41. *Origanum vulgare* 'Aureum' Golden marjoram #	●				●	●	●		●		
42. *Passiflora edulis* Passionfruit				●	●			●			
43. *Pelargonium tomentosum* Peppermint-scented geranium #	●				●	●		●			
44. *Pennisetum alopecuroides* Fountain grass	●				●			●			
45. *Petroselinum crispum* Curled parsley #	●				●	●					
46. *Phalaris arundinacea* var. *picta* Ribbon grass #	●				●			●			
47. *Rosa* 'Fru Dagmar Hastrup' #	●				●	●			●		
48. *Rosa* 'Iceberg' #		●		●	●						●
49. *Rosmarinus officinalis* Rosemary	●				●				●		●
50. *Salvia elegans* Pineapple sage	●				●			●			
51. *Salvia leucantha* Mexican sage #	●				●				●		
52. *Santolina chamaecyparissus* Silver santolina #	●				●			●			●
53. *Stachys byzantina* Lamb's ear	●				●				●		
54. *Tagetes lucida* Sweet-scented marigold	●				●			●		●	
55. *Thymus* x *citriodorus* Lemon-scented thyme #	●				●				●		
56. *Thymus serpyllum* Wild thyme #	●				●			●			
57. *Tropaeolum majus* Nasturtium #	●				●	●	●	●			
58. *Vaccinium* species Blueberry #	●	●	●			●					
59. *Viola odorata* Sweet violet #	●				●	●	●	●			
60. *Wisteria sinensis* Chinese wisteria				●	●	●			●		●

\# This symbol indicates that the species or one of its varieties or cultivars has a Royal Horticultural Society Award of Merit.

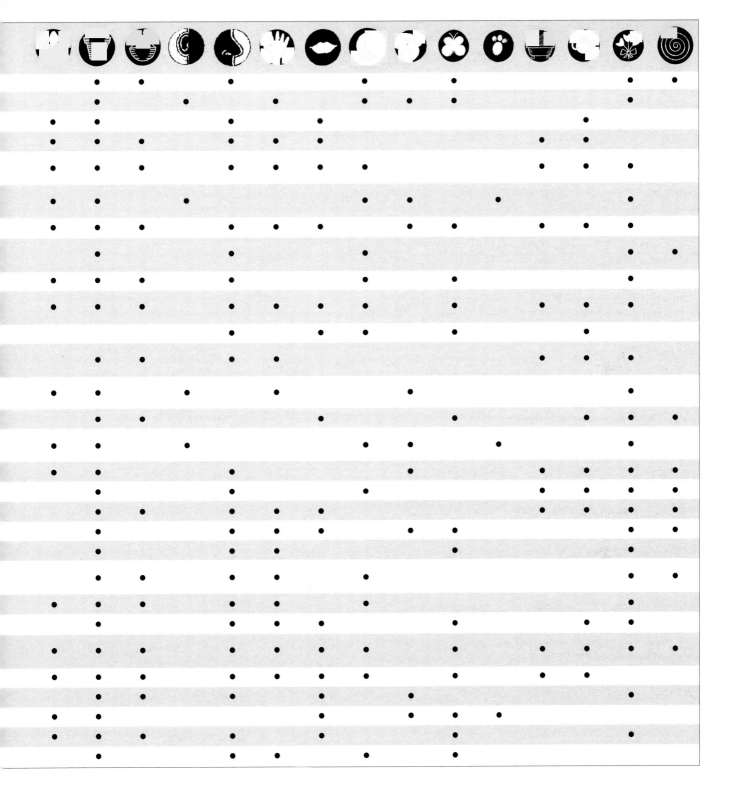

Descriptions

1. *Abelia* x *grandiflora*

Sun. 2 m (6½ ft)

Abelia is a decorative evergreen shrub which is barely seen in summer for the profusion of small white bells. These have a faint, sweet perfume and are attractive to butterflies and bees. When the flowers fall, they leave their dusky-pink sepals behind, and these last into winter. It is a quick-grower which forms a dense thicket of canes, providing nesting places and shelter for small birds. A beautiful golden-leaved form is also available. Both can be clipped into a rounded bush or formal hedge.

2. *Acmena smithii*

Sun or shade. 50 cm–12 m (20 in–40 ft) depending on variety

The lillypilly is a lush-leaved native of eastern Australia's rainforest gullies. Fluffy white flowers in the warmer months of the year attract butterflies, and are followed by masses of pink fleshy fruits through autumn, winter and spring. These are relished by birds and other fruit-eating wildlife, and can be eaten by humans, too — however, they taste best when made into a delicious chutney or jam. In the wild, lillypilly is often seen as a tree, but in gardens it is usually grown as a medium-sized shrub. It is amenable to clipping and makes an excellent hedge. There are an increasing number of dwarf varieties, including the bun-shaped cultivar 'Hedgemaster' which grows only 1 m (3 ft) high.

3. *Actinotus helianthi*

Sun. 50 cm (20 in)

Flannel flower is a short-lived butterfly-attracting herb, and one of Australia's most beautiful little natives. The whole plant, from the deeply divided grey-green leaves to the daisy-like flowers, is covered in soft woolly white hairs. The flowers, which appear in spring and summer, seem pressed from creamy-white felt. Beautiful at dusk, they are a flower-arranger's delight, fresh or dried. Flannel flower can be grown from seed. It needs well-drained, sandy soil.

4. *Aloysia triphylla* (syn. *Lippia citriodora*)

Sun or part-shade. 2–3 m (6½–10 ft)

Lemon-scented verbena is a must for the fragrant garden. Its leaves are bright green and pointed and when crushed they release a mouthwatering lemon fragrance. They can be used fresh or dried, in teas, or added to baths or potpourris. The pale lilac flowers in small spikes on delicate stems are also fragrant, and can be used in summer posies. Where winters are cold it is best grown in a pot and overwintered in a greenhouse. It is hardy to −5°C (23°F).

5. *Angelica archangelica*

Sun or shade. 1.5 m (4½ ft)

Angelica is an impressive biennial herb with large serrated leaves. Every part of the plant is edible and sweetly aromatic: the hollow stems are juicy with a celery-like texture; the young leaf stalks have a muscat flavour; the young leaves can be finely sliced and added to salads; the roots can be cooked like a vegetable; and the seeds, like the rest of the plant, can be used to make herbal tea blends. The seeds have also been used in perfumery and as a flavouring in liqueurs.The heavy crop of seeds which follow the green flowerheads make good pickings for birds. Angelica prefers light shade and a rich, moisture retentive soil, but it will grow in full sun if the soil is damp. It survives temperatures to −45°C (−49°F).

6. *Anigozanthos* species

Sun. 25 cm–2 m (10 in–6½ ft), depending on variety

Kangaroo paws are a remarkable group of evergreen perennials native to Western Australia. They have sword-shaped leaves in grassy clumps, and interesting felty flowers which resemble the shape of a kangaroo's paw. These are usually held above the foliage and come in a dazzling colour range including lime-green, orange, pink, brown, golden-yellow and brilliant red. Nectar-feeding birds the world over find them irresistible, and they make handsome and long-lasting cut or dried flowers. Bright yellow-flowered *A. manglesii* 'Bush Dawn', one of the best for cutting, is ideal for colder climates. Kangaroo paws make excellent pot specimens and dwarf varieties can be grown in window boxes.

7. *Argyranthemum frutescens* (syn. *Chrysanthemum frutescens*)

Sun or part-shade. 40 cm–1 m (15 in–3 ft)

The marguerite daisy, or daisy bush, is a rounded evergreen shrub. In warm temperate climates, given a sunny location, it flowers almost year-round. But the real show is in mid-summer, when the attractive, heavily divided leaves are almost hidden behind the display. The best known marguerite daisy is a single white with a yellow centre. But there are also yellow, cream and pink varieties, in singles and doubles. Dwarf varieties are suitable for hanging baskets and window boxes. In climates with temperatures below 0°C (32°F), it is used as an annual, or cuttings are taken in autumn and kept in a greenhouse over winter.

8. *Artemisia* 'Powis Castle'

Sun. 50–60 cm (20 in–2 ft)

This silvery mound deserves a place in every garden. The filigree fronds, which are fragrant to touch, are ethereal by night and twilight, especially when combined with white flowers. It makes an excellent filler in posies, blending with almost every plant in the garden. This cultivar of artemisia has the best foliage of all, but no flowers. If you want butterflies, and similar feathered leaves, plant *A. arborescens* which grows to 1.5 m (4½ ft).

9. *Banksia ericifolia*

Sun or part-shade. 4 m (13 ft)

Heath banksia, a bushy Australian native shrub, is a superior plant for wildlife gardens, offering food, protection and nesting sites. The impressive, nectar-laden orange–red flower spikes attract butterflies, birds and many other small creatures when they appear in autumn, winter and spring. The seed which follows feeds another legion of creatures. Birds often seek refuge, or build nests within the thicket of its inner branches. The upright flowers are wonderful in bold flower arrangements. Closely-related *Banksia* 'Birthday Candles', with flower spikes 40 cm (15 in) or more high, is an outstanding cut-flower plant.

10. *Brachyscome multifida*

Sun or part-shade. 20 cm (8 in)

Brachycome, or cut-leaf daisy, is a dainty Australian native groundcover with fine ferny leaves and tiny daisy flowers. The blooms appear for much of the year, with the best flush in spring and summer. Full sun ensures the best crop of flowers. The most common form has mauve flowers with a golden centre, but pink, purple and yellow varieties are also available, as is white, to catch the moonlight. The leaves are fragrant when touched. A regular light clipping with hedging shears keeps it compact, and helps to release the fruity scent. It spreads up to a metre (3 ft) wide. Brachycome tolerates a wide range of soil conditions.

the pleasure plant index

11. *Bracteantha bracteata*
(syn. *Helichrysum bracteatum*)

Sun. 20–75 cm (8 in–2½ ft)

The everlasting daisy is a frost-hardy, often short-lived, Australian perennial. It is sometimes called paper daisy or strawflower on account of its stiff, papery petals. These crackle when rubbed and make superb fresh or dried flowers. A vast array of colours include rich reds and browns, and pastel shades of pink, cream and yellow. One of the best cultivars, especially by night, is 'White Monarch' which has white petals and an orange centre. Butterflies and insects are attracted to everlasting daisy, so it often brings insect-eating birds as well.

12. *Buddleja davidii*

Sun. 1.5–3 m (4½–10 ft)

Buddleia, often called butterfly bush, is possibly the world's greatest butterfly magnet. The arching flower spikes, made up of masses of tubular flowers, have a sweet honey scent and are white, cream, orange, mauve, purple or deep purple–red, depending on the variety. They appear over many months but are most prolific in summer. Their delicious sweet honey scent wafts around the garden, and can be brought inside for fragrant posies. Nectar-feeding birds sometimes feed on buddleia's flowers and, if they are left to fade, they will then feed seedeaters as well. Dwarf varieties which grow only 1.5 m (4½ ft) high are excellent for small spaces. Prune hard in spring.

13. *Callistemon citrinus* cvs

Sun. 1–4m (3–13 ft)

Crimson bottlebrush is an outstanding shrub for birds, providing a feast of seed, nectar and insects. It is shared with other nectar-seekers, too, such as bees, butterflies and small animals. The stiff, narrow leaves have a fresh lemon-eucalyptus scent

when crushed. Many cultivars are available, the most popular being 'Endeavour' or 'Splendens' which has brilliant red spikes almost year-round, with most impressive displays in late spring and autumn. There is a white-flowering form for night-shining flowers.

14. *Chamaemelum nobile*
(syn. *Anthemis nobilis*)

Sun. 15 cm (6 in)

Lawn chamomile is a low-growing groundcover with tiny daisy flowers. The foliage has a luxurious mossy texture and a fragrance which, to my nose, has a squeeze of lemon, a dab of musk and a sprinkling of pine needles. It tolerates light foot traffic and can be used for paths and lawns. The flowers, fresh or dried, are infused in boiling water for teas, or sprinkled on bathwaters, and are reputed to calm and soothe. The pompom flowers of the cultivar 'Flore Pleno' are excellent for night gardens, while non-flowering 'Treneague', a neat prostrate form, is often used for lawns. Lawn chamomile is hardy to −23°C (−9°F).

15. *Citrus sinensis*

Sun. 3–4.5 m (10–15 ft)

The orange tree is an outstanding pleasure plant. It is fragrant in all its parts, from the citrus-scented foliage, and sweet spring blossoms to the sensational fruit itself. Tangy, delicious and nutritious, it can be enjoyed freshly cut or juiced. A few shavings of the outer peel in a pot of tea transports the brew into another stratosphere of taste and fragrance. Like all citrus, orange trees attract butterflies. It can be grown in large tubs, and can also be espaliered. Among the best varieties for taste are 'Washington Navel' and 'Valencia'. Orange trees need a frost-free position, so the protection of a glasshouse is needed where winters are cold.

16. *Cymbopogon citratus*

Sun. 1 m (3 ft)

Lemongrass has thin strappy leaves which form dense clumps that rustle in the wind. Both the stem bases and leaves are lemon-scented and the leaves release their fragrance when stroked or crushed. Either can be used in cooking and teas. It is a tropical plant but grows in a wide range of climates. Where winters are cool to cold it should be brought indoors for the coldest part of the year. It makes an attractive pot specimen.

17. *Daphne odora*

Part-shade. 1 m (3 ft)

Daphne is a small evergreen shrub with a wonderful wafting perfume by day and night. The flowers appear in winter, and are usually purple, although deep wine-red and white varieties are also available. The flowers can be brought indoors for decoration and may fill the room with fragrance. Daphne requires a well-drained soil in light shade. The species grows best where temperatures are above 4°C (39°F), though some sources suggest that it survives temperatures to −10°C (14°F). The cultivar 'Aureomarginata', which has gold-edged leaves, is hardy to −15°C (5°F).

18. *Dianthus plumarius* cvs

Sun or part-shade. Up to 25 cm (10 in)

Cottage pinks are evergreen perennials with small carnation-like blooms held on branched stems above attractive blue–grey tufts. The vast range of cultivars range in flower colour including pink, mauve, maroon, crimson and white, in single, double or fringed varieties. These attract butterflies, and appear mainly in spring and summer. Their sweet-clove perfume is accentuated in still, warm places, such as next to a brick-paved path. 'Mrs Sinkins' has heavily scented double white flowers in the middle of summer, making it a good choice for night gardens. Cottage pinks prefer well-drained, slightly alkaline soil and are hardy to −34°C (−30°F).

19. *Eriostemon myoporoides*

Sun or part-shade. 2 m (6½ ft)

Waxflower is a small Australian native shrub which is smothered in white or pink star-shaped flowers in winter and spring. The petals have an interesting waxy texture, and the leaves are fragrant when crushed. It is highly attractive to butterflies, and a single plant can provide non-stop picking flowers for months on end. An excellent cultivar called 'Profusion' has an exceptional display of white flowers and apple-scented leaves. Waxflower is hardy to both drought and light frosts, but it needs good drainage.

20. *Foeniculum vulgare*

Sun. 1.5 m (4½ ft)

Fennel, with its feathery, plume-like fronds, is an outstanding foliage plant which offers a sensory feast of touch, smell and taste. It has a distinct aniseed flavour. It is also a favourite food plant for butterfly larvae. The cultivar 'Purpureum', known as bronze fennel, has bronze–brown foliage and is particularly elegant. In cool climates, fennel dies down in winter and returns to form a new clump in spring. It is hardy to −29°C (−20°F).

21. *Freesia refracta*

Sun or part-shade. 30 cm (12 in)

Freesias have grass-like leaves and tubular flowers which, if you choose the right ones, have the most ambrosial of fragrances. Steer clear of the modern, brightly coloured hybrids. Most have a disappointing fragrance and lack the secret drop of honey which can be sucked from their base. Freesias make

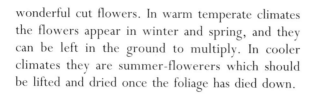

wonderful cut flowers. In warm temperate climates the flowers appear in winter and spring, and they can be left in the ground to multiply. In cooler climates they are summer-flowerers which should be lifted and dried once the foliage has died down.

22. *Gardenia augusta* (syn *G. augusta* 'Florida' and *G. jasminoides*)

Part-shade. 1 m (3 ft)

Gardenia is a small evergreen shrub with glossy green leaves. Its sweetly perfumed double white flowers open pure white and yellow with age. If it is given a warm temperate climate, shelter from the hottest sun of the day and a rich, well-drained, slightly acid soil, it will flower from late spring to autumn, spilling its perfume into the air day and night. There are a number of cultivars, though few rival the species for profusion and length of flowering. *Gardenia augusta* 'Radicans', a useful groundcovering cultivar, is one of the better cultivars. It grows 50 cm (20 in) high and up to 2 m (6½ ft) wide and can be used in large hanging baskets and window boxes. All gardenias live happily in pots and in cool climates they are used as a conservatory plant.

23. *Grevillea* 'Robyn Gordon'.

Sun. 1.5 m (4½ ft)

This is one of the best plants for attracting nectar-feeding birds. It is a good size for most gardens and forms a dense rounded mound of heavily divided foliage — a beautiful backdrop to the bright red flowers which are scattered over the shrub for most months of the year. Like other grevilleas, it is also attractive to butterflies and other nectar-feeding wildlife. It does well in pots and can be brought indoors. It is worth noting, however, that for some people, it can cause skin rashes. Grevilleas need a well-drained soil.

24. *Grevillea rosmarinifolia*

Sun. 2 m (6½ ft)

Rosemary grevillea is a bushy evergreen shrub which provides birds and other wildlife with nectar-rich flowers, as well as shelter and nesting sites within its spiky cover of needle-like leaves. The most common variety has red flowers for most of the year, and there are also pink and cream forms. It makes an excellent hedge and can be clipped formally. This is one of the more frost-hardy species of grevillea. Dwarf varieties are also available.

25. *Helianthus annuus*

Sun. Up to 3 m (10 ft)

Sunflowers, with their huge flowers and bright yellow petals, rarely fail to capture the imagination. They are annuals, usually planted by seed, with an enormous selection of heights, as well as flower types and colours to choose from. The flower's nectar-rich centre attracts all sorts of flying creatures, including butterflies and small birds. If left to dry, the flower also feeds seed-eating birds, as well as yourself. But, if you want seed, be sure to choose single-flowering varieties — that is, ones with a single row of petals. Many doubles are infertile and never set seed. Sunflowers are exceptional cut flowers.

26. *Helichrysum petiolare* (syn. *H. petiolatum*)

Sun or shade. 75 cm (2½ ft)

Silver helichrysum and gold helichrysum (*H. petiolare* 'Limelight') have round, felty leaves which are lovely to touch. As daylight fades, they come to life. Gold helichrysum in particular seems to capture even the faintest glimmer of moonlight. They are also invaluable posy plants, blending with almost every other flower and foliage. Silver helichrysum can be planted in full sun or shade, while gold helichrysum prefers a little shade during summer. Neither is frost-hardy, so in cool climates they should be kept in a greenhouse throughout winter or cuttings should be taken in autumn. Prune lightly often.

27. *Heliotropium arborescens*

Sun or part-shade. 40 cm (15 in)

Heliotrope, sometimes known as cherry pie, has flowers which have a mouth-watering vanilla fragrance. The flower colour varies from pale to rich mauve depending on the variety. The green- and gold-leaved varieties emit the strongest, most wafting perfume, while the purple-leaved variety has a faint scent which must be enjoyed up-close. The flowers bring bees and butterflies, and can be used in posies, but it is best to cut them early in the morning, and gently crush the stem's end with a small hammer. The shade-loving gold-leaved form has pale-coloured flowers and is excellent in the night garden. Heliotrope grows best in mild climates with temperatures over 5°C (41°F).

28. *Jasminum officinale*

Sun or part-shade. 6 m (20 ft) or more

Poet's jasmine has exquisitely perfumed starry white flowers over many months, mostly during the warmest part of the year. These make fragrant additions to posies and bath waters, and can be used in tea-making — either added sparingly to the brew, or stored with tea leaves to imbue it with aromatic flavour. Aromatherapists use the essential oil of this species for its sedative qualities. Though it is a climber, it is rather sprawling and develops a wonderful gnarled trunk. It is best where it can roam free — over an arbour, arch or wall, for example. In cooler climates it needs a warm sheltered position.

29. *Lavandula angustifolia*

Sun. 30 cm–1 m (12 in–3 ft), depending on variety

Lavender is another plant which is used in aromatherapy for its soothing and calming properties, and it is this species, English lavender, from which the essential oil is extracted. Like so many lavenders, it has soft grey–green leaves and flower clusters in a spike at the end of long stems, which bring butterflies, bees and other small nectar-lovers. All parts of English lavender are edible but only a little is needed as the taste is very strong. It can also be used in posies, or to scent bathwaters. The flowers appear in spring and summer. There are mauve, pink and white varieties, and a number of dwarf cultivars. *L. angustifolia* 'Nana Alba', a dwarf white cultivar, is ideal for night gardens. English lavender is hardy to −15°C (5°F), but it is often short-lived in warm, humid climates.

30. *Lavandula dentata*

Sun. 1 m (3 ft)

French lavender has attractive toothed leaves and soft mauve flowers. The flowers appear for most of the year, with an impressive flush in winter and spring, and bring butterflies and bees to the garden. They can also be dried, but are best used in fresh floral arrangements. Both flowers and leaves can be added to bath waters. It should not be eaten, however. This is one of the best lavenders for humid warm temperate climates.

31. *Leptospermum petersonii*

Sun or part-shade. 4 m (13 ft)

The Australian native lemon-scented tea tree has a beautiful paperbarked trunk, an intense lemon fragrance when its leaves are crushed, masses of white starry flowers in spring and summer for butterflies and flower arranging, and plenty of seed for birds. It grows into a tall shrub or small tree.

32. *Lobularia maritima*

Sun. 20 cm (8 in)

This wonderful little plant gives so much for so little. Low hedges along garden beds and paths are quickly established. All you need is a good sprinkling of compost and a couple of packets of seed, and within weeks they will be amongst the garden's star performers. Each lacy mound of honey-scented flowers becomes a nectar-fest for bees and butterflies. By night the white-flowering variety is lit up like a fairyland metropolis. Violet, lilac, rose, carmine and cream flowers are also available, and can be woven together to make an intricate floral carpet. For non-stop blooms for months on end, clip lightly with hedging shears and sprinkle with fertilizer every four weeks when they are at their peak in spring and summer. They are short-lived, so replace them regularly.

33. *Lunaria annua*

Sun or shade. 75 cm (2½ ft)

Honesty is another plant which can be grown from seed. It grows in almost any position and is extremely hardy. The dainty flowers attract butterflies and are followed by one of the most interesting seed heads in the plant world. Round, with a stiff papery texture, they make interesting noises when they clap together. Birds may peck at them for the free seed treat that waits inside. Or peel off the outer casing yourself to reveal the shiny see-through discs. These are excellent for flower arrangements, especially in front of a sunny window.

34. *Malus pumila*

Sun. 3 m (10 ft)

There are literally thousands of varieties of apple in a huge range of flavours, colours, shapes, and sizes. Each has its own individual aroma, often with sweet, spicy, floral or berry-like notes. Most apples are not self-fertile — two different varieties are needed for cross-pollination. A large garden is needed for two full-sized trees, but dwarf and upright varieties are also available, and some of these are also suitable for pots. Espalier and duo or trio planting (see page 28) are other space-saving ways to grow apple trees. As with all fruit trees, choose a variety which does well in your area, and be sure to taste the fruit before you buy — some are grown for cooking or ciders rather than eating. Apples prefer a climate where winters are cool to cold, and summers are mild. They survive temperatures to −40°C (−40°F).

35. *Mentha x piperita*

Part-shade to shade. 30 cm (12 in)

Peppermint has the freshest scent of any herb — clean, delicate, cooling and refreshing. Like English lavender and poet's jasmine, it, too, is valued for its essential oil, which is extracted from the leaves. Often recommended as a relaxant, peppermint tea is one of the best herbal brews, served hot or iced; and peppermint leaves sprinkled in bath water elevates a simple soak to a soothing, aromatic experience. As with other mints it throws out runners and tends to take over. Either grow it in a large pot, sunk into the ground if you like, or give it its own garden bed, perhaps with other mints. It thrives in moist or boggy soil.

36. *Mentha suaveolens* 'Variegata'

Sun or shade. 30 cm (12 in)

Variegated applemint is an irresistible plant, for its beauty as well as its taste and fragrance. The leaves are softly woolly and pale green edged in cream. As the name suggests, they have a sharp apple scent which is an excellent addition to hot or iced teas. The variegation in the leaves is accentuated at dusk and by moonlight. Applemint is loved by flower arrangers. It grows in sun or shade, though a little shade is best — the white part of the leaf tends to scorch in strong summer sun. It is not quite as invasive as other mints but it is still wise to keep it contained or give it its own space.

37. *Miscanthus sinensis* 'Zebrinus'

Sun or part-shade. 1.2–1.5 m (4– 4½ ft)

Zebra grass is a tall and elegant clumping grass with upright, arching, rustling leaves. The horizontal bands of yellow, not unlike the markings on a jungle animal, make the leaves stand out at night. It holds its feather-like flower heads high above the foliage, and feeds birds with its seed. When planted near water, it provides shelter for small amphibious animals. The leaves look good in arrangements with plants such as arum lilies, *Kniphofia* and *Strelitzia*. It is hardy to −23°C (−20°F).

38. *Monarda didyma*

Sun or part-shade. 60–90 cm (2–3 ft)

Bergamot is a beautiful old-fashioned herb. Its soft green leaves have a delicious fragrance — a subtle combination of mint, lemon and aniseed. When infused, they make delicious Oswego tea, and they can also add a refreshing fragrance to a bath. The brilliant red summer flowers can be used in posies, and are sweet to taste. They are adored by butterflies, honey-eating birds and bees — in fact, it is often called bee balm. Pink and mauve flowering forms are also available. Bergamot prefers moist soil and is hardy to −34°C (−29°F).

39. *Murraya paniculata*

Sun or part-shade. 2–4 m (6–13 ft)

Orange-scented jessamine is a rounded evergreen shrub with dark green glossy leaves. In the warm months of the year it produces masses of creamy-white star-shaped flowers which have a sweet orange-blossom fragrance. These catch the moonlight, and can also be used for picking. It makes an excellent perfumed hedge.

40. *Nepeta* x *faassenii*

Sun. 20 cm (8 in)

Catmint is a spreading perennial with grey–green leaves and pale lavender flower spikes. The foliage is aromatic but somewhat pungent. The short flower spikes, which hover above the foliage during the warmest months, are the real attraction. They bring the garden to life with bees and butterflies, and can also be used as an accompaniment in posies. This dwarf variety is arguably the best of all catmints. It spreads to around 50 cm (20 in) wide and is hardy to −29°C (−20°F).

41. *Origanum vulgare* 'Aureum'

Sun. 15 cm (6 in)

Golden marjoram, or golden oregano as it is sometimes called, is a perennial herb which spreads to make a luscious golden rug. It is fragrant to touch, delicious to eat and glows under the light of the moon. Its pink, lipped flowers bring butterflies. The green-leaved species, *O. vulgare*, was traditionally used in perfumery, and modern herbalists find it useful as a relaxant and for treating all manner of conditions including sluggishness and insomnia. It is always nice to brush past or collect sprigs for cooking, baths, teas or posies. It spreads 60 cm (2 ft) or more and is one of the easiest plants to grow.

42. *Passiflora edulis*

Sun. 3 m (10 ft) or more

Passionfruit is surely one of the world's most exquisite tastes, and the vine from which it comes is extremely decorative and useful. The large, glossy leaves are a perfect backdrop for the white and purple flowers, which feature an explosion of spidery stamens. It is one of the very best plants to grow for butterflies — the adults sip the nectar and the young caterpillars enjoy the leaves. The flowers are followed by round black–purple fruit which wrinkles when it is ready to eat. The tangy pulp can be scooped out and eaten fresh, or added to iced teas, perhaps with a splash of champagne. It needs a sunny position and is ideal in warm to tropical climates. 'Nelly Kelly' is a grafted cultivar which resists disease and tolerates climates with light frosts.

43. *Pelargonium tomentosum*

Sun or part-shade. 1 m (3 ft)

Peppermint-scented geranium has thick, felty leaves with a sweet peppermint aroma when touched. It spreads to form a downy mound and can be used as a spillover along low brick walls. Unlike most other sun-loving scented geraniums, it is happiest in light shade. A few leaves in a sealed container will scent sugar cubes for herb teas. In climates where winters are cool, it can be brought indoors from autumn until early summer.

44. *Pennisetum alopecuroides*

Sun or part-shade. 1 m (3 ft)

Fountain grass, a native of Australia and Asia, is a neat tussocking grass with pink flowers as soft as a kitten's tail. These attract seed-eating birds and are decorative cut fresh or dried. The long arching leaves gently rustle in the wind. The clumps should be divided every few years, removing any dead leaves. It has a strong tendency to self seed, so it is often used in drifts or mass plantings. 'Hameln', a dwarf non-seeding variety, is the best choice for cool climates. It grows to 40 cm (15 in) high and is hardy to −23°C (−9°F).

45. *Petroselinum crispum* (syn. *P. hortense*)

Sun or part-shade. 45 cm (18 in)

Curled parsley is a well-known, nutritious, biennial herb, but it deserves attention for many other reasons, too — it adds a luscious ferny element to posies, gives iced teas a sparkle, can be used in hot herbal tea blends and is a favourite food plant for butterfly larvae. Use it wherever you would grow a low, clipped hedge. Along a path, for example, it creates a verdant, lacy edge which is always a pleasure to clip. It grows best in a moist, well-drained soil with plenty of compost and manure.

46. *Phalaris arundinacea* var. *picta*

Sun or part-shade. 1 m (3 ft)

Ribbon grass, or gardener's gaiters, is an upright-growing grass with lovely striped leaves of pale green and white. It enjoys a boggy spot and is ideal for nearby water where it provides shelter to small creatures. The soft white flower spikes which appear in summer are attractive to birds. It spreads quickly, so plant it where it can roam free, mark out its space with underground barriers, or plant it in a bottomless bucket. The leaves are tuneful in a strong breeze, and make the most of the moonlight. It is hardy to −34°C (−29°F).

47. *Rosa* 'Fru Dagmar Hastrup'

Sun or part-shade. 1 m (3 ft)

This is an excellent compact rose. The fragrant pale pink flowers appear almost continuously from late spring to autumn, when they are joined by the shining tomato-red rose hips. These are beautiful in autumn posies and can be used to make rose hip tea. This is one of the easiest roses to grow. It is highly resistant to disease and tolerates drought and neglect. It makes an excellent flowering hedge, and requires little maintenance. It has a spread of around 1.2 m (4 ft) and is hardy to −45°C (−49°F).

48. Rosa 'Iceberg'

Sun or part-shade. 1.5 m (4½ ft)

This Floribunda rose, one of the world's most popular roses, can be bought as a shrub, climber or standard. The double white blooms appear almost all year round, particularly in the warmer months, making it an excellent plant for the night garden. The fragrance is best enjoyed up-close, so place it within easy reach of the nose. It makes a beautiful long-lasting cut flower and the petals can be infused in boiling water to make rose petal tea. The shrub form of 'Iceberg' is suitable for informal hedges.

49. Rosmarinus officinalis

Sun. 1 m (3 ft)

Rosemary is an aromatic evergreen shrub which deserves a position next to the door or path where its foliage can be brushed on passing. In cooking, it is often combined with equally strong flavours such as garlic, red wine and game dishes. Small amounts, of half a teaspoon or less, make a fragrant addition to herbal teas, but the true power of its aroma is unleashed in the steamy waters of the bathtub. Rosemary is ideal for formal hedges, while a prostrate cultivar called 'Prostratus' (syn. *R.o. lavandulaceus*) is ideal for cascades over low walls.

50. Salvia elegans (syn. S. rutilans)

Sun or part-shade. 1 m (3 ft)

Pineapple sage is a highly attractive small bushy shrub with masses of beautiful scarlet flowers and fresh green leaves which have the delicious scent of ripe pineapples. The flowers, which appear mainly in summer, have a sweet fruity taste, and also lure butterflies, bees and, like all red-flowering salvias, nectar-feeding birds. In climates with mild to warm winters it is a perennial. In cooler climates it is often treated as an annual and left to die down when the temperature drops; it sometimes re-emerges with warm weather in the following season. Alternatively, it may be kept in a greenhouse or conservatory over winter.

51. Salvia leucantha

Sun. 1 m (3 ft)

Mexican sage is a small shrub with narrow grey–green, silver-backed leaves. The flowers begin in early summer and continue through autumn and into winter. They are velvet-textured in mauve and white on long white woolly stems and attract butterflies and bees. The flowers can be cut for posies and may also be dried. The leaves are aromatic but the scent is somewhat pungent. In winter it should be cut almost to ground level. It is hardy to −5°C (23°F).

52. Santolina chamaecyparissus

Sun. 30 cm (12 in)

Silver santolina is a small shrub with foliage which is among the closest to white. If placed within reach, it is irresistible, perhaps because it seems so un-plant-like. Though the tiny jagged leaves, crowded together in tight masses, have a dry crusty appearance, the touch sensation is soft and pleasing. It makes one of the best low hedges for sunny places, and the aromatic foliage makes it pleasant to clip. Such hedges can play a practical role in the garden at night, acting as beacons either side of a path, for instance. It has yellow button flowers on stems above the foliage in summer. It is hardy to −15°C (5°F).

53. Stachys byzantina (syn. S. lanata and S. olympica)

Sun. 20 cm (8 in)

Lamb's ear is a ground-covering perennial which provides the garden with one of its most wonderful touch sensations. Its leaves are silver and furry above and white and woolly below. They have a faint aroma — fresh, mint-like and a little sweet. The flowers are woolly, too, and are rose–lilac in colour. Both leaves and flowers can be used in flower arrangements, fresh or dried. Lamb's ear, like silver santolina, is luminescent by moonlight, as is the lime-gold cultivar 'Primrose Heron'. It is hardy to −29°C (−20°F).

54. *Tagetes lucida*

Sun. 60 cm (2 ft)

Sweet-scented marigold is a large herbaceous perennial herb with golden flowers and toothed leaves which release a delicious tarragon-like aniseed fragrance when brushed or crushed. Steeped in water, the leaves make a deliciously sweet tea, and it can be used in cooking as one would use French tarragon. The flowers, too, are edible and can be sprinkled over salads. Appearing in autumn, they make a brilliant display in a vase. It dies down completely in winter to return again each spring.

55. *Thymus* x *citriodorus*

Sun. 25 cm (10 in)

There are 300 or more species of thyme. Many have their own individual fragrant notes, but at the heart of the scent there is always that unmistakable thyme aroma. Lemon-scented thyme takes up very little space — it grows in a small bun shape — but it gives so much. It is a close relative of common thyme (*T. vulgaris*) which is used in cooking, and it, too, can be used anywhere a hint of lemon is desired. The lilac flowers, in clusters at the end of shoots, are brimming with nectar for bees and butterflies. It looks beautiful in a posy, especially the silver-variegated 'Silver Queen', and golden-leaved 'Aureus'. These cultivars are also the best choice for night gardens. Lemon-scented thyme makes an excellent low hedge, and the range of colours makes it one of the best choices for knot gardens. All members of the thyme family need a sunny, well-drained position, and grow best with a gravel mulch. It is hardy to −29°C (−20°F).

56. *Thymus serpyllum*

Sun. 10 cm (4 in)

Wild, or creeping thyme is the best thyme for creating fragrant carpets, lawns, paths and seats. Low-growing and dense, it spreads by setting down roots as it grows, yet it is easily controlled. Wild thyme offers exciting possibilities for colourful murals, because of the wide variety in flower colour, as well as leaf colour and texture. Flower colours include white, pink, lilac–pink, magenta and crimson; leaf textures vary from smooth to woolly, and the foliage colour may be green, grey–green or golden. The white flowers of the form 'albus' shine by moonlight. Wild thyme is also useful between stepping stones, in paving cracks, or spilling over paths. It is hardy to −29°C (−20°F).

57. *Tropaeolum majus*

Sun or shade. 30 cm (12 in)

Nasturtium is a spreading annual with circular leaves and brightly coloured flowers which run the gamut of the warm colour spectrum from palest lemon, through yellow and orange, to rich ruby-red. Leaves may be green or variegated, and some are almost entirely creamy-white. Both the leaves and flowers are edible, and are beautiful in salads. Up-close, the flower trumpets reveal a sweet nectar scent which explains their popularity with bees and small nectar-feeding birds. A collection of nasturtium flowers in varying hues lasts a few joyful days in a small vase. Nasturtium is an excellent groundcover and spillover in sun and shade. It is especially useful for difficult spots where nothing seems to grow. It is easily grown from seed.

58. *Vaccinium* species

Sun or part-shade. 45 cm–6 m (18 in–20 ft), depending on variety

The blueberry is an attractive shrub with delicious fruit which often appears in the first year of planting. Within six years, one blueberry plant may produce literally bucketfuls of small, round, blue–purple berries in clusters along the branches, and a healthy shrub can produce crops for 50 years or more. The shrub itself is highly ornamental with dark green leaves, arching canes and, in spring, clusters of small pink–white flowers which are similar to lily of the valley. Most varieties are deciduous, or semi-deciduous in warmer climates, and many have brilliant autumn leaf displays. Small growing species — such as *V. angustifolium*, which grows only 45 cm (18 in) tall — are ideal for small gardens and pots. Blueberry attracts butterflies, and birds and other fruit-eaters enjoy the fruit. Why not share the crop and place fine net mesh only over those you want to keep? Blueberry needs an acid soil so, at planting, add half a bucket of peat moss to the hole and mulch with a thick layer of pine needles. Most varieties need a cool to cold winter, and some are hardy to −45°C (−49°F), however, cultivars are also available for warmer climates.

59. *Viola odorata*

Sun or shade. 15 cm (6 in)

Sweet violet, a close relative of the pansy, is a small perennial with heart-shaped leaves and sweetly perfumed flowers. It gradually spreads to form a dark green carpet with purple flowers on delicate wands in winter and spring — and often at other times of the year as well. Pink, white, apricot and blue flowering varieties are also available. These may differ in scent, some being sweeter than others. Their 'faces' are lovely in small flower arrangements. Both flowers and leaves are edible —the blossoms are rich in vitamin C and the leaves in vitamin A. The flowers can also be captured in ice cubes to be floated in iced tea, or used to scent sugar, and an infusion (tea) of sweet violet flowers is said to have a mild sedative and laxative effect. The leaves are a favourite food source for butterfly larvae. Sweet violet enjoys winter sun and summer shade — beneath deciduous trees, for example. It is happiest in cool, moist, well-drained places. Use sweet violet in paving cracks, as an edging along paths and steps, under shrubs and roses, and as a spillover amongst other plants in pots and hanging baskets. In pots and in the garden they look beautiful tucked in amongst other small plants; in the garden especially, sweet violet is a merry mingler, weaving itself in and around other things, and doing the gardener's work of filling small spaces which need to be filled. A twice-yearly clipping with the hedging shears and a sprinkling of rotted or pelletised chicken manure make sweet violet flourish. It is hardy to −23°C (−9°F).

60. *Wisteria sinensis*

Sun or part-shade. 15 m (50 ft), unpruned

Wisteria is *the* plant for pergolas and tunnels, and this species, Chinese wisteria, is the easiest to grow. In late winter or early spring exquisitely fragrant racemes, up to 30 cm (12 in) long, hang from the roof like chandeliers. In summer it creates a cool, shaded sanctuary and in winter it lets the sun shine in through its interesting gnarled stems. The flowers are followed by seed pods which have a furry texture. In smaller gardens it can be grown as a standard in a large pot, or trained up a sturdy pole to form a 'tree' in the centre of the lawn. Mauve is the most common flower colour, but a white cultivar is also available. Chinese wisteria is extremely vigorous and should be pruned after flowering. It is hardy to −18°C (0°F). The hardier Japanese wisteria survives temperatures to −34°C(−29°F).

Sources

Nurseries

Many of the following nurseries offer an inspiring experience, along with their exciting range of plants. Some have display gardens and mail order catalogues which may be free on request. A few are mail order only, as indicated.

Australia

VICTORIA

Australian native plants

Austraflora Nursery & Gardens
7–9 Belfast Road, Montrose 3765
Phone (03) 9728 1222

Perennials, herbs, bulbs and roses

Country Farm Perennials
Laings Road, Nayook 3821
Phone (056) 28 4202

Herbs, perennials, fragrant plants and roses

Otway Herb Nursery
Biddles Road, Apollo Bay 3233
Phone (052) 37 6318

Seeds, perennials, bulbs, roses, shrubs and trees, all by mail order

Diggers Mail Order
'Heronswood', 105 Latrobe Parade, Dromana 3936
Phone (059) 87 1877

Perennials and rock plants by mail order

Norgates Plant Farm
Blackwood Road, Trentham 3458
Phone (054) 24 1265

Perennials by mail order

Lambley Nursery
'Burnside', Lesters Road, Ascot 3364
Phone (053) 43 4303

Water and wetland plants by mail order

Dragonfly Aquatics
RMB AB 366, Colac 3250
Phone (052) 36 6320

NEW SOUTH WALES

Australian native plants and grasses

Wirreanda Nursery
169 Wirreanda Road, Ingleside 2101
Phone (02) 450 1400

Scented plants of all kinds

The Fragrant Garden
Portsmouth Road, Erina 2251
Phone (043) 67 7546

Perennials, old-fashioned roses, fragrant shrubs and trees

Colonial Cottage Nursery
62 Kenthurst Road, Dural 2158
Phone (02) 654 1340

Perennials, herbs, scented geraniums, and old-fashioned roses

Honeysuckle Cottage Nursery
Lot 35, Bowen Mountain Road, Bowen Mountain, via Grosevale 2753
Phone (045) 72 1345

Perennials, some shrubs and trees

Belrose Nursery
Bundaleer Road, Belrose 2085
Phone (02) 450 1484

AUSTRALIAN CAPITAL TERRITORY

Wide range of perennials, and selected roses and shrubs

Albert's Garden
9 Beltana Road, Pialligo 2609
Phone (06) 248 0300

WESTERN AUSTRALIA

Australian native plants, especially those of Western Australia

George Lullfitz Nursery
Corner Caporn Street and Honey Road, Wanneroo 6065
Phone (09) 405 1607

Perennials, herbs, shrubs, roses and fruit trees

Lavender Blues Nursery
176 Anzac Road, Mount Hawthorne 6016
Phone (09) 444 4826

QUEENSLAND

Pennyroyal Herb Farm
Penny's Lane, Branyan, Bundaberg 4670
Phone (071) 55 1622

Native plant specialist

Utingu Native Plant Nursery
95 Birdwood Road, Holland Park 4121
Phone (07) 3397 5706

SOUTH AUSTRALIA

Camellias, azaleas, perennials, roses, fruit trees, scented shrubs and trees

Newman's Nursery & Topiary Tea House
North East Road, Tea Tree Gully 5097
Phone (08) 264 2661

TASMANIA

Unusual perennials, shrubs and trees

Woodbank Nursery
RMB 303, Kingston 7150
Phone (002) 39 6452

New Zealand

Very wide general range of plants

Palmers Gardenworld
Corner Shore and Orakei Roads, Remuera
Phone (09) 524 4038

Perennials, herbs, old-fashioned roses

Gethsemane Gardens
27 Revelation Drive, Christchurch
Phone (03) 326 5848

Canada

Wide range of plants

Weall & Cullen
784 Sheppard Avenue East, North York, Toronto, Ontario M2K IC3
Phone (416) 225 7705

Rose specialists

Pickering Nurseries
670 Kingston Road, Pickering, Ontario L1V 1A6
Phone (905) 839 2111

United Kingdom

Most of the following nurseries have catalogues and mail order, and will ship plants to other European countries.

Extensive plant range, including many Australian natives

> Burncoose & South Down Nurseries
> Gwennap, Redruth, Cornwall TR16 6BJ
> Phone (01209) 86 1112

Very wide range of plants

> Bressingham Gardens
> Bressingham, Diss, Norfolk IP22 2AB
> Phone (01379) 68 8133

Wide range of fruit trees (including 75 apple trees)

> Brogdale Horticultural Trust
> Brogdale Road, Faversham, Kent ME13 8XZ
> Phone (01795) 535 462

Mainly perennials, as well as plants for special situations

> The Beth Chatto Gardens Ltd
> Elmstead Market, Colchester,
> Essex CO7 7DB
> Phone (01206) 822007

Herbs, old-fashioned roses, salvias and cool conservatory plants

> Hollington Nurseries
> Woolton Hill, Newbury,
> Berkshire RG15 9XT
> Phone (01635) 25 3908

Conservatory plants

> Long Man Gardens
> Lewes Road, Wilmington, Polegate,
> East Sussex BN26 5RS
> Phone (01323) 87 0816

Helpful Information

Wildlife Organisations

The following organisations provide brochures, information or publications to help you turn your backyard into a wildlife habitat.

Australia

> Wildlife Information & Rescue Service (WIRES)
> PO Box 260, Forestville, NSW 2087
> Phone (02) 9975 5567

> Gould League of Victoria
> Genoa Street, Morrabbin, Victoria 3189
> Phone (03) 9532 0909
> Fax (03) 9532 2860

New Zealand

> Royal Forest & Bird Protection Society of New Zealand
> PO Box 631, Wellington
> Phone (04) 385 7374 Fax (04) 385 7373

Canada

> Sierra Club, Canada
> 1 Nicholas Street, Suite 420, Ottawa, Ontario K1N 7B7
> Phone (613) 214 4611

> Canadian Wildlife Federation
> 1673 Carling Avenue, Ottawa, Ontario K2A 3Z1
> Phone (613) 721 2286

United Kingdom

> Butterfly Conservation
> PO Box 222, Dedham, Colchester, Essex CO7 6E4
> Phone (01206) 322 342 Fax (206) 322 736

> Royal Society for Nature Conservation (RSNC)
> The Green, Witham Park, Waterside South, Lincoln LN5 7JR
> Phone (01522) 544 400

> Royal Society for the Protection of Birds (RSPB)
> The Lodge, Sandy, Bedfordshire SG19 2DL
> Phone (01767) 680 551

Other Useful Contacts

Membership of the following organisations gives you access to information about the best plants for your local conditions and how to grow them successfully.

Australia

> The Society for Growing Australian Plants
> 3 Currawang Place, Como West, NSW 2226
> Phone (02) 528 2683 Fax (02) 528 2683

> Wildflower Society of Western Australia
> PO Box 64, Nedlands, WA 6009
> Phone (09) 383 7979

United Kingdom

> Hardy Plant Society
> Little Orchard, Great Comberton, Pershore, Worcs WR10 3DP
> Phone (01386) 71 0317

Index to Plants